Biotechnology

Brookings Dialogues on Public Policy

The presentations and discussions at Brookings conferences and seminars often deserve wide circulation as contributions to public understanding of issues of national importance. The Brookings Dialogues on Public Policy series is intended to make such statements and commentary available to a broad and general audience, usually in summary form. The series supplements the Institution's research publications by reflecting the contrasting, often lively, and sometimes conflicting views of elected and appointed government officials, other leaders in public and private life, and scholars. In keeping with their origin and purpose, the Dialogues are not subjected to the formal review procedures established for the Institution's research publications. Brookings publishes them in the belief that they are worthy of public consideration but does not assume responsibility for their accuracy or objectivity. And, as in all Brookings publications, the judgments, conclusions, and recommendations presented in the Dialogues should not be ascribed to the trustees, officers, or other staff members of the Brookings Institution.

Biotechnology

Implications for
Public Policy

Papers by ALBERT GORE, JR.

JOSHUA LEDERBERG

JOHN D. DINGELL

LEWIS THOMAS

JAMES J. FLORIO

GEORGE B. RATHMANN

SIMON A. LEVIN *&* MARK A. HARWELL

BERNADINE HEALY BULKLEY

presented at a conference at the Brookings Institution,

on January 15–16, 1985

Edited by SANDRA PANEM

THE BROOKINGS INSTITUTION
Washington, D.C.

Copyright © 1985 by
THE BROOKINGS INSTITUTION
1775 Massachusetts Avenue, N.W.
Washington, D.C. 20036

Library of Congress Catalog Card Number 85-48176
ISBN 0-8157-6903-2

9 8 7 6 5 4 3 2 1

About Brookings

THE BROOKINGS INSTITUTION is a private nonprofit organization devoted to research, education, and publication in economics, government, foreign policy, and the social sciences generally. Its principal purpose is to bring knowledge to bear on the current and emerging public policy problems facing the American people. In its research, Brookings functions as an independent analyst and critic, committed to publishing its findings for the information of the public. In its conferences and other activities, it serves as a bridge between scholarship and public policy, bringing new knowledge to the attention of decisionmakers and affording scholars a better insight into policy issues. Its activities are carried out through three research programs (Economic Studies, Governmental Studies, Foreign Policy Studies), a Center for Public Policy Education, a Publications Program, and a Social Science Computation Center.

The Institution was incorporated in 1927 to merge the Institute for Government Research, founded in 1916 as the first private organization devoted to public policy issues at the national level; the Institute of Economics, established in 1922 to study economic problems; and the Robert Brookings Graduate School of Economics and Government, organized in 1924 as a pioneering experiment in training for public service. The consolidated institution was named in honor of Robert Somers Brookings (1850–1932), a St. Louis businessman whose leadership shaped the earlier organizations.

Brookings is financed largely by endowment and by the support of philanthropic foundations, corporations, and private individuals. Its funds are devoted to carrying out its own research and educational activities. It also undertakes some unclassified government contract studies, reserving the right to publish its findings.

A Board of Trustees is responsible for general supervision of the Institution, approval of fields of investigation, and safeguarding the independence of the Institution's work. The President is the chief administrative officer, responsible for formulating and coordinating policies, recommending projects, approving publications, and selecting the staff.

Editor's Preface

MORE than a decade has passed since the first experiments that laid the foundation for the genetic revolution of the 1970s were performed. Genetic engineering promised inexpensive and plentiful biological products for pharmaceutical, agricultural, and petrochemical use. Biotechnology's first products have now appeared on the market. Although the promise of the technology is even more compelling than in those early days, questions persist about the best way to manage biotechnology's development. A particular focus is the risk of releasing genetically engineered microorganisms into the environment. That debate raises the generic issues of how the federal government can consistently regulate new technologies, foster preeminence of U.S. industry, and safely encourage technological innovation.

In the hope of fostering informed public debate, the Brookings Institution convened a symposium on January 15 and 16, 1985, to address the public policy implications of biotechnology. This volume, in the Brookings Dialogues on Public Policy series, reports the results of that conference and contributes to the development of sound public policy. The viewpoints from several sectors are presented, providing the perspectives of those who practice the technology and those who consume it.

Many individuals contributed to the success of the conference and the completion of this publication. At Brookings, the organizational and editorial efforts of Julia Sternberg and Diana Coupard were invaluable. Theresa B. Walker edited the manuscript for publication. Robert Nicholas, Subcommittee on Science and Technology Oversight of the House Energy and Commerce Committee, assembled an exemplary planning committee and developed an informative and exciting program. The Brookings Institution is grateful to the members of the planning committee for their guidance. The support of the Allied Corporation, the Conservation Foundation, the Department of Agriculture, E. I. du Pont de Nemours & Company, the Dow Chemical Company, the Environmental Protection Agency, the Environmental Policy Institute, the Food and Drug Administration, the Industrial Biotechnology Association, the Monsanto Agricultural Products Company, the Natural Resources Defense Council, and Genentech, Inc., is gratefully acknowledged.

Sandra Panem

November 1985
Washington, D.C.

Contents

SANDRA PANEM

Introduction

SANDRA PANEM

IN THE 1970S, the biological sciences experienced a technical revolution. The revolution, known popularly as biotechnology or genetic engineering, allowed development of unique tools that can be used to produce rare biological products in large quantity, with high purity and at low cost. The technology also permits the development of exquisitely precise and sensitive monitoring methods to detect diverse molecules, such as heavy metals, dioxins, PCBs, and other toxic wastes, at exceptionally low concentrations.

The techniques can be broadly applied. Initially, obvious opportunities were recognized in the chemical, pharmaceutical, agricultural, and petrochemical industries. The commercial potential has shifted the focus of basic research from the public to the private sector and forced a reevaluation of the roles of government, academe, and industry in the research and development of new high technologies.

The first commercial products of the new biotechnology are now appearing. Their entry into the marketplace occurs during a time of clear public mistrust of the ability of government to appropriately assess, foster, and regulate new technologies and their products. The current period is also one in which the adversarial climate that has long characterized regulation is being questioned.

The tenor of this climate can be caught in several excerpts from a 1984 Brookings Institution Dialogue, *Public Policy, Science, and Environmental Risk*. Consider, for example, these comments from a former director of life sciences in the White House's Office of Science and Technology Policy, "The current process is basically adversarial. We know in advance that almost every significant issue will end up in the courts, and so we start with the most extreme positions."[1]

1. Denis Prager, "Science and Environmental Risk: Policy Issues," in Sandra Panem, ed., *Public Policy, Science, and Environmental Risk* (Brookings, 1983), p. 27.

Similarly, a former congressional staff director observed

> The counterproductivity of the adversarial route is perhaps most clearly shown by the Reagan Administration's loss of credibility in environmental and health-protection policy. The 1980 election provided a public mandate and a golden opportunity to rationalize the setting of health and environmental standards in this country. . . . A quiet and scientifically solid approach to seeking appropriate revisions in regulatory law and policy could have gathered broad support and brought both political and technically oriented rewards. However, by allowing its approaches to regulatory reforms to be encumbered by strong ideological and adversarial extremes, the administration tragically disenfranchised itself as a credible partner in true problem solving approaches. In fact it has probably set the stage for another backlash of excessive zeal in environmental regulation.[2]

Consequently, the current development of regulations for the new biotechnology demands attention for three different reasons. First, the problems of biotechnology are unique, intrinsically interesting, and important. Second, the development of responsible federal regulation of biotechnology is a test of the ability of the U.S. system to manage the problems of a powerful new technology in society's best interest. Third, the development of a framework for regulatory decisionmaking in biotechnology before the appearance of a large number of products requiring regulation provides a unique opportunity. This is the opportunity to develop a flexible and nonadversarial regulatory system in which the producers, consumers, and regulators participate in establishing a regulatory process.

What is biotechnology? There are many answers to this question. Broadly defined, biotechnology is the application of biological processes for commercial use. In the context of the current regulatory debate, biotechnology concerns the commercial development of products employing the techniques of recombinant DNA technology (gene splicing, gene cloning) and of hybridoma technology (monoclonal antibodies). Yet the fuzzy line between these new procedures and those well established before the 1970s, has forced the reexamination of previous regulatory practices. Thus tension exists between the regulation of new versus old commercial biological enterprises. The question, "Is there anything new and special about biotechnology?" is continually raised.

2. Thomas H. Moss, "Risk Assessment and the Legislative Process," in Panem, ed., *Public Policy, Science, and Environmental Risk*, p. 22.

This question is fundamental because its answer will provide guidance about whether new regulations and even new regulatory institutions are required. As the papers in this volume attest, there is a consensus that the new techniques of genetic engineering are very powerful, can be applied in many industries, and will result in the appearance of many new products. Yet the debate on whether the products are, for regulatory purposes, significantly different from previous products has yet to yield a consensus.

One common theme in this debate centers on whether products or processes should be regulated. Debate surrounding this point should be easily resolved when a problem in semantics about what is *process* regulation and what is *product* regulation is clarified. All chemical, pharmaceutical, and agricultural regulation in the United States is product oriented. Part of product-oriented regulation is consideration of the process by which the product is produced. Process consideration is necessary if for no other reason than to assess quality. For example, the presence of contaminants in a particular product will differ depending upon the manufacturing processes employed. A second way in which product-oriented regulation considers process is in the regulation of products used in the manufacturing steps. When this is understood, the debate over regulating products or processes is seen as a straw man argument.

The definitions of what kinds of biotechnology products should be regulated, and by whom, are central issues concerning biotechnology. As the contents of this volume indicate, there is currently no consensus on what constitutes biotechnology for regulatory purposes.

Developing regulations

Commercial interest in the new techniques of biotechnology has developed rapidly. The lack of a well-defined federal regulatory strategy for the new products is not a reflection of the establishment being asleep at the switch—but rather a reflection of the sudden merger of basic and applied science. Traditionally, basic research has not been subject to the formal regulatory structure that has characterized the efforts of applied research.

Scientific discovery and its technological applications can be divided into three distinct phases. Phase one includes events that lead to the discovery of a phenomenon, its description, and its mechanistic explanation. Before genetic engineering, phase-one work was done at universities, in research institutes, or, occasionally, in industrial facilities.

Phase two is a period of application, in which processes are developed to exploit phenomena discovered in phase one. In this traditional stage, before genetic engineering, work was done predominantly in the commercial sector and in academic settings in which process development was the research subject (for example, schools of agriculture and departments of applied microbiology).

Phase three is a development period in which work is confined to manufacturing, packaging, and marketing the products derived from phases one and two. Clinical trials and collection of data to fulfill federal requirements for drug approval are also performed during this stage, as are efforts to meet premanufacturing data requirements for chemical and pesticide registration. Phase-three work has occurred and continues to occur within the private sector.

Before the late 1970s, the three stages were separated both by the work site (academe versus private industry) and in time. It was not unusual for the time lag between initial discovery of a phenomenon, its translation into a product, and the appearance of a product in the marketplace to be several decades or more. This time factor is largely responsible for the perception that fundamental or basic research is different in content, as well as displaced from, applied research and development.

With genetic engineering came a tremendous change that can be viewed as a "time collapse." The fundamental experiments with recombinant deoxyribonucleic acid (DNA) techniques were performed between 1971 and 1973, the first insulin gene was cloned in 1977, and the first genetically engineered insulin was approved by the Food and Drug Administration in late 1982. Less than nine years had elapsed between phase one and the completion of phase three, including the time-consuming clinical trials for testing insulin. In contrast, it took thirty-two years to complete phase one through phase three on the first heart pacemaker. There are comparable examples with agricultural products. The effects of time collapse on the biological research community is elegantly addressed in this volume in the remarks by Lewis Thomas.

In view of the speed with which genetic engineering is coming of age, its newness, and the slow process by which federal conventions are established, it is not surprising that a regulatory system has yet to be put in place. The process is further complicated by a unique element of biotechnology—the generation of viable products. Although viable microbial products have been commercialized in the past, widespread use of new techniques suggests that an increasing number of viable products will be developed.

One way in which applied and basic research has been traditionally distinguished is by the scale of the enterprise. For example, a basic research lab might use a ten-liter fermentation apparatus, but an applied research lab might employ a fifty-thousand-liter apparatus. Problems of scale have provided a convenient measure for establishing points at which formal regulation occurs. This is based on the concept that great increases in scale are accompanied by risks that do not occur on a small scale and that require attention by the federal establishment.

An example of scale as a means of determining when federal regulation is appropriate can be seen with small-scale R&D field testing of pesticides. In the past, testing of an experimental chemical pesticide has been exempt from the formal requirement of an experimental use permit under the Federal Insecticide, Fungicide, and Pesticide Act, in a field of less than ten acres. Yet with viable pesticides, the difference between one hundred square feet and ten acres is not really a matter of scale but a matter of time. The number of organisms placed on a one-hundred-square-foot patch may well multiply to that needed for ten acres in a few hours or days. In addition, unlike nonviable pesticides, a viable product cannot be recalled from the field if it is found to have adverse qualities. This changes the questions to be asked about a product's "transport and fate" in the environment. The problems unique to evaluating viable biotechnology products for use in the environment are the subject of the remarks by Simon A. Levin and Mark A. Harwell.

Although there is consensus that field testing of microbial pesticides is different from that for chemical agents, the current decision by the Environmental Protection Agency to eliminate the exemption for genetically engineered organisms in fields of less than ten acres has come under dispute. The debate exemplifies the tensions of regulatory policy toward old and new technologies. Some have argued that there is no need to develop new regulatory strategies because the problems associated with biotechnology products are analogous to those previously managed. In support of this view, many cite regulatory procedures for new drugs and biorational pesticides. However, while microbial pesticides have been used since the 1940s, only fourteen products have been registered. In contrast, in the past year alone, the Environmental Protection Agency has had serious premanufacturing consultations with at least six companies seeking to develop genetically engineered pesticides. This illustrates an additional component of the issue of scale—types of products that in the past appeared infrequently are now likely to become common.

There was consensus that it is in everyone's best interest to strike the correct balance between regulating for safety and not overregulating to the point of stifling innovation. The development of a consistent and rational federal regulatory policy for biotechnology is the continuing subject of deliberation of the White House's Cabinet Council Working Group on Biotechnology. The working group was formed in 1984 to serve as an interagency forum in which the executive branch of government could develop a federal biotechnology policy. The working group is chaired by the White House Office of Science and Technology Policy. It is also the subject of a *Federal Register* notice dated December 31, 1984, "Proposal for a Coordinated Framework for Regulation of Biotechnology."[3] Bernadine Healy Bulkley's comments concern that notice, which includes an eighteen-page list of different federal statutes that may be applied to biotechnology. Thus the task is not to generate regulatory authorities (many of which are on the list), but rather to determine the most rational way to implement these authorities in a consistent manner.

Which agencies have overlapping jurisdictions? How can interagency tensions be identified and resolved? How can agencies share their expertise and experience to enhance consistency and lack of duplication? Are there gaps in regulatory authorities? If so, how can any gaps be closed? One possibility is that new legislation may be needed. However, a point of consensus at the conference was that new legislation was not immediately needed. Additionally, any suggested new legislation would benefit from the case-by-case experience that is now accumulating.

One conference participant questioned the efforts of the Office of Science and Technology Policy by asking: "was it appropriate for the cabinet council to operate on the premise that biotechnology is good?" This question is central to any discussion of public policy surrounding a technology. Is it the technology, or the technology's use, that is value laden?

Scientists and policymakers

Throughout the conference tensions were evident that may help to explain the diversity of opinions expressed on how federal biotechnology policy should be developed. A fundamental tension occurs between basic research scientists and policymakers about the role of the nonscientist in decisions about science and technology. This tension arises first from the difficulty of separating expert technical judgment from policy judgments, and second from the difficulty of expressing technical problems in generally

3. *Federal Register*, vol. 49 (December 31, 1984), pp. 50856–907.

accessible lay language. Some of these "cross-cultural" issues have been cogently captured by Judge David L. Bazelon in "Governing Technology: Values, Choices and Scientific Progress":

> When scientists participate in the public debate over biotechnology— as I hope they will—they must keep in mind the specific role that they play. They are not, unless so designated, the policy makers. Their role is not to make conclusions concerning the appropriate trade-offs among risks, but rather to make clearer what the estimated trade-offs are. What the public needs most from an expert, biologists included, is his wealth of intermediate observations and conceptual insights adequately explained. Decisions of the ultimate questions must be left to the public decision-making process. . . .
>
> Scientists who appear in the public arena all too often focus on little more than making conclusory pronouncements. . . . They tell us a particular innovation is safe, rather than *how safe* and *why*. They ignore the basic fact that a conclusion that a technology is "safe" reflects a host of value choices about the relative importance of such diverse concerns as the health of a particular industry or company, the severity of the problem addressed by the technology, and the value of the things that the technology might harm.[4]

Judge Bazelon's observations focus on the distinctions between the processes of risk assessment and risk management as they are used by federal regulatory agencies. Only those with technical expertise can adequately assess risk. In contrast, the management of risk requires consideration of additional factors and is amenable to broad public discussion. The decisionmaker is frequently unsure if the expert is presenting only a technical judgment, or, alternatively, a judgment that reflects the expert's views as a citizen. In a parallel consideration, the expert may perceive that the translation of his technical judgments into lay terms is an act of distortion and may therefore maintain that only those with technical expertise can make rational risk-management judgments. This mutual skepticism between scientists and policymakers frequently leads to mutual distrust.

The decisionmaker must believe that he or she is being presented only with dispassionate facts. The scientist must feel that the technical realities are realistically presented. These needs are further complicated in the case of contemporary biotechnology. As the papers in this volume show, there is currently a consensus that the data and tools for definitively assessing all of biotechnology's risks do not exist. Certainly there is no basis on which to quantify

---

4. David L. Bazelon, "Governing Technology: Values, Choices, and Scientific Progress," *Technology in Society*, vol. 5, no. 1 (1983), p. 19.

risk assessments or ensure zero risk. The acknowledgment of this situation strengthens the natural skepticism between the scientist and the policymaker and sometimes leads to an overly emotional debate.

Assessing risks

The classic distinctions between fundamental and applied research in biotechnology are no longer clear. Furthermore, the potential consequences of biotechnology that deserve public policy attention do not allow the traditional distance between science and the public to be respected.

This confrontation between the research enterprise and the inquiring public policy community is exacerbated by an additional tension that exists within the scientific community. There is an interdisciplinary tension between molecular biologists and ecologists. This is evident in the assessment of the risks associated with biotechnology—especially where the new products of genetic engineering will be deliberately released into the environment. Daniel L. Hartl sums up contrasting images of the ecologist and the molecular biologist in his comments in this volume.

Experts disagree on the extent and the way to assess the risks of the new products of biotechnology. Part of the disagreement derives from the differences in interdisciplinary perspectives noted by Hartl. But part of the problem, as explained by a conference participant, is that different things are known about the different aspects of what is now called biotechnology. Perhaps one ought to classify this field of biotechnology. The approach to risk will differ, depending on where on the continuum of knowledge the area falls. The difference in state-of-the-art knowledge about the different areas of biotechnology also causes a divergence of opinion on what would constitute adequate resources for filling in the "knowledge gaps."

Despite disagreement among experts, there are some points of consensus. First, there is no such thing as zero risk. Second, the odds are that most proposed products will not present major risks. Third, products of biotechnology must be evaluated on a case-by-case basis. Fourth, more research relevant to biotechnology risk assessment is required.

Many questions arise about research and risk assessment. Who should determine what research is needed? Who should fund the work? Where should it be done? What constitutes an adequate predictive capability? How would one go about developing it? How will the United States produce the number and quality of scientists necessary to do the research? Is there a need for new educational programs to allow scientists to perform the ecological evaluations that are needed?

Until there is more experience, a generic risk-assessment protocol cannot be written. Yet one can begin to articulate the questions that must be considered in evaluating the safety of a biotechnology product.

Public education and participation

A common theme and point of consensus was that good communication with, and participation by, the public is needed for effective regulation of biotechnology. To ensure these, the public must be kept informed in a way that can be understood. Acknowledging the difficulty in communication about complex technical problems is not an excuse for shutting the public out of the discussion, as mentioned by many throughout the conference.

Besides educating the general public, it is essential to ensure that information is provided to decisionmakers such as those in Congress. What are the sources of technical information for members of Congress, and how accurate and adequate are they? Are there ways to improve the flow of this type of information into the decisionmaking process? The comments in this volume of Douglas Costle, former administrator of the Environmental Protection Agency, are especially lucid on this subject.

The Asilomar experience

A historic event in the history of biotechnology—the 1975 Asilomar Conference—is especially important in understanding the need to emphasize the role of the public in the contemporary debate on regulating biotechnology. The Asilomar experience was extensively mentioned by many participants at the conference and is offered by some as a model for dealing with current problems.

In 1975 the widespread experimentation with recombinant DNA technology was beginning in biomedical research laboratories. In response to concerns within and outside the research community, a conference was held at Asilomar, California, to discuss potential hazards of the technology. The results of deliberations by scientific leaders at that meeting was to call a moratorium on certain kinds of experiments until their safety could be ensured by the results of "paradigm" experiments.

An outgrowth of the Asilomar meetings and subsequent experiments was the development of guidelines by the National Institutes of Health Recombinant DNA Advisory Committee (RAC). The National Institutes of Health organized this committee. It is composed of scientists who serve as consultants, to judge, or peer review, the scientific merit of research proposals submitted that request funding for experiments utilizing recombinant DNA technology. The RAC guidelines, although binding only on NIH grantees, have been voluntarily adopted by many research establishments, including industrial ones, who were not seeking NIH funds. Consequently, in the absence of any federal guidance for the use of genetic engineering in commercial settings, the RAC became a de facto regulatory agency. Since the mid-1970s the guidelines have been extensively altered, and for the most part, relaxed. Relaxation came with the understanding that many biomedical R&D applications as practiced in university settings do not constitute hazardous work.

It is important to emphasize two points about the Asilomar experience: what it was and what it was not; and, why the process is only partially applicable and appropriate to the current debate on regulating biotechnology. At Asilomar responsible scientists voluntarily paused in their work to assess the risks associated with a powerful new technology. They formulated guidelines for safe work with a few select microorganisms and a few techniques to be used in defined research laboratory settings. The experiments were designed to test "the safety of biotechnology" as a research technique and were not tests of the safety of all applications of genetic engineering. For example, the questions surrounding deliberate release of microorganisms into the environment were not addressed by these exercises. Many of the issues highlighted by addresses in this volume were as difficult to approach in 1975 as they are now. It is important to emphasize that the questions resolved through the Asilomar experience do not speak to current environmental concerns.

Furthermore, the Asilomar meeting did not include widespread public participation, and was not concerned with widespread industrial-scale work and the issues of commercialization now under discussion. The meeting did not deal with questions that now must be faced by the regulatory authorities under law—because, in essence, the subject in 1975 was academic R&D. Now with commercialization the subject of biotechnology and its implications has broadened.

The techniques of biotechnology are no longer the domain of only an elite, academic research community. The Asilomar participants are now only one of many groups whose voices must be heard in debate. As laudable and unique as the Asilomar exercise in self-regulation was, it is not suited to the problems of the 1980s. Yet this realization does not negate the important lessons of Asilomar: case-by-case analysis is required; regulatory guidelines will need to change as experience with technology expands and therefore must be flexible; and science is not irretrievably set back by pausing for short periods for reasoned discussion.

Discussion of the Asilomar experience also emphasizes the rapid growth of genetic engineering and its applications. Although the de facto regulatory function played by the RAC is no longer appropriate for the needs of the 1980s, the lessons of the RAC are valuable. Expert technical advice is needed for risk assessment.

The current challenge

The following papers and comments describe a spectrum of opinions about the potential of biotechnology to improve, as well as to threaten, the quality of society's health and environment. Perhaps the most pressing current challenge is for the federal government to develop a framework for use in making rational decisions about the issues raised by biotechnology. The intent of this volume is to serve as a record of one part of the public debate that will contribute to that framework's development, and to stimulate the debate's continuation.

A Congressional Perspective

ALBERT GORE, JR.

BIOTECHNOLOGY has captured the public's imagination by providing a dramatically increased understanding of how life's processes work. Biotechnology holds the promise of new medicines and procedures for health care; new varieties of crops that withstand natural stresses and grow with less use of herbicides and pesticides; and new industrial chemicals, which could be environmentally preferable to existing chemicals.

While the potential of biotechnology is viewed with excitement, the power of this technology may provoke a certain amount of apprehension. Now, as the products of biotechnology are on the verge of commercialization, it is vital to ensure that development follows a safe course without unnecessarily burdensome regulation. This is the great challenge that makers of public policy are facing today.

Public apprehension about technology is not unique to biotechnology. I think there is a growing apprehension about technology in general. When people are confronted with the visions of new products and miraculous discoveries coming from new technology, they often wonder what is on the other side of the coin.

The potential of biotechnology

I think many Americans feel concerned about new technologies these days. Perhaps their sentiments were first expressed by Nietzsche when he said that science is fundamentally nihilistic. Many are concerned that the world as we know it will be reshaped by new discoveries in this field.

The apprehensions grow out of the experience of nuclear technology. It is instructive to look at how unrealistic many of the fears about nuclear technology were, and how some of the concerns that were not considered turned out to be very threatening indeed.

In a documentary film, "The Atomic Cafe," about the early days of nuclear weaponry, a scientist expresses a patently ridiculous

12

concern that the pending test of a hydrogen bomb at Bikini Atoll could theoretically touch off a chain reaction in the world's oceans which would dry them up, leave the ships at the bottom of the sea, and humanity without a source of water. This was followed by more thoughtful scientists clucking that this was patently ridiculous. I think many of the concerns expressed during the infancy of biotechnology were in the same category. They were patently ridiculous. There was a mathematically quantifiable risk. It was so tiny that it should have been ignored, but it could not be.

On the other hand, in the example of nuclear weapons, society might have focused less on these wild, unrealistic hypotheticals and more on what the real impacts of nuclear technology were likely to be. What of its potential to completely change the world? Then society surely would have insisted that public policymakers conduct policy over the last thirty to forty years in a very different way than it has been conducted. Look at the mess into which we have gotten ourselves.

I believe that biotechnology has more potential to reshape the world as we know it than any other technology besides nuclear power. This time, public policy implications should be handled a little bit better than the implications of technology have been handled in the past.

If the promise of representative democracy is to be redeemed, therefore, society must stimulate and sustain a wide public debate including scientists, business leaders, public policymakers, academics, and others, in a discussion of what the true implications of this technology are; what choices have to be made; and how those choices can best be made.

There are three broad areas of concern in biotechnology and public policy. The first deals with the information that comes from biotechnology—just the information, not its application. There have been early public policy implications in issues like genetic screening in the workplace. For example, is it fair to deny someone a job if that person's genetic heritage gives him or her a 5 to 10 percent elevated risk of contracting an occupational disease or sustaining an occupational injury? Collective common sense, built upon the experience of past generations, does not provide a ready answer for that question. And the legal system responds to the question with a shrug of the shoulders, more or less.

As more information becomes available, very challenging public policy issues are going to arise. What will biotechnology's impact be on the insurance industry? For example, people are now grouped into very large categories and the risk is spread among them. What will happen when microcategories are created in the actuarial tables as a result of the more accurate description of the specific risk each individual faces becomes possible?

New information is increasing at a rapid rate. Some estimates have put the doubling time now at six months. A witness at one of the hearings held by the Senate Subcommittee on Toxic Substance and Environmental Oversight compared the growth of biotechnology information with the first pictures of the earth taken from satellites. He said the first pictures showed us the outline of the continents. As technology progressed, the major river systems and smaller lakes became visible. Then city streets appeared. Now, the individual mailboxes along the streets of every city in the world can be seen, and soon it will be possible to tell if the flag on the mailbox is up or down.

The human genome can be seen as a large set of continents. Very soon, the major tributaries will be identified. A few of the individual mailboxes have already been identified. But before very long, all of the mailboxes, all of the individual genes that make up the genome of the human species, whether the flag is up or down, and whether the gene is turned on or off will be discernible. The implications of having that information are enormous. There is an obligation to choose to act or not to act upon that information.

Another concern is the use of biotechnology to produce new substances, to alter existing plants and animals for the benefit of humanity, and, particularly, to introduce these new products into the environment.

The application of biotechnology to human beings raises another area of concern. This category has the most profound implications. The first approved genetic therapy procedures are soon to take place. When one acquires the ability to change the blueprint of human life, then the potential grows and public apprehension grows.

Congress has already dealt with several of these issues. Specific areas of congressional interest have included the public health risks of laboratory research using recombinant DNA techniques; commercialization of academic, biomedical research and the implications of university ties to commercial biotechnology companies; the ethical implications of these early applications of genetic engineering to human beings; the promotion of U.S. biotechnology in international competition; the agricultural applications of biotechnology and the potential risks and benefits of environmental applications of genetically engineered organisms; genetic therapy and its implications; alternative reproductive technologies; genetic screening; and the regulatory structure that the government of the United States should organize to cope with these questions.

Discussions of regulating this technology have occurred during the past decade. The debate over the safety and health risks of laboratory research was perhaps the most notorious. Legislation that would have regulated research involving recombinant DNA was introduced in the Ninety-fifth Congress. Several bills proposed the establishment of many new federal regulations and suggested approaches ranging from declaring a total moratorium on research until completion of a risk assessment, to establishing licensing and certification procedures for researchers and laboratories. During the congressional session of 1977 and 1978 alone, sixteen different bills dealing with recombinant DNA were introduced, several of which would have made the National Institutes of Health (NIH) guidelines mandatory for private industry. Yet, to date, no federal legislation directly regulating recombinant DNA research has ever been passed.

There are several reasons for this fact, the chief one being the establishment of the National Institutes of Health's Recombinant DNA Advisory Committee, (RAC), and this committee's development of the "Guidelines for Research Involving Recombinant DNA Molecules." The Asilomar Conference, which led to these developments, and the existence of the RAC, are extraordinary examples of the willingness of the scientific community to regulate itself in the face of scientific uncertainty. The important lesson about these past events is that public acceptance of this kind of laboratory research came only after extensive public debate, in which the scientific community played a leading and responsible role.

The concern about the potential safety hazards of the new genetic engineering procedures resulted in restricting the application of these procedures for a short time. Some research projects were postponed, while others were performed using highly inconvenient containment measures. But the RAC guidelines for acceptable laboratory practices proved to be highly flexible. As knowledge and confidence in the safety of recombinant DNA laboratory research grew, the public's perceptions of risk decreased. Today, most laboratory research is exempt from such restrictions. In the long run, the research got done, and the public trust in science was maintained.

Some members of the scientific community look back on the

early days of restrictions with bitterness. One prominent molecular biologist recently referred to the events of the 1970s as "the cycle of anxiety, sterile debate, bureaucratic regulation, and eventual recovery." Apparently, this scientist, and possibly others, felt that biotechnology had paid its debt to society and should now be left alone to pursue commercialization unhindered and without further needless restrictions.

Unfortunately, it is precisely the fact of commercialization that drastically changes the present picture. Congress is no longer simply dealing with scientific research. Rather, Congress is now confronted with the need to ensure that commercial products coming out of biotechnology, particularly those designed for environmental applications, receive adequate and publicly acceptable review for the protection of public and environmental health and safety.

In the debates of the 1970s, a consensus developed among scientists that a cautious approach was reasonable until more was known. Eventually the scientific consensus shifted, at least among molecular biologists, away from the need for caution and toward a more relaxed view of safety measures. It is important to recognize, however, that while this consensus on the safety of laboratory research did develop, it did not and does not extend to the question of environmental applications of genetically engineered organisms. This whole issue was sidestepped when the National Institutes of Health guidelines prohibiting deliberate release, and minimizing the risk of accidental release, were universally accepted.

Congressional responsibility

In June of 1983, the Subcommittee on Toxic Substances and Environmental Oversight held the first congressional hearings on the release into the environment of genetically altered organisms. These questions were addressed:

—What are the risks and benefits of deliberate release?

—What is the state of the art in the ability to predict the environmental consequences of such a release?

—How well positioned are the federal agencies—the Environmental Protection Agency, the Department of Agriculture, and the National Institutes of Health—to make decisions regarding releases into the environment of new genetically altered organisms?

—Are the laws adequate; is there a way to provide better coordination and more adequate scientific expertise?

The subcommittee drew the following conclusions. There are many potential benefits to be derived from such releases. A small number of such releases may, however, present a risk of significant adverse consequences. The ability to do risk assessments, to describe and evaluate the likelihood of any particular risk in this area is not well developed at all. No federal agency has both the expertise and the legal authority to make decisions concerning the release of genetically altered organisms into the environment on a commercial scale.

The subcommittee did not call for the creation of a new agency or any new legislation. The subcommittee did recommend that an interagency committee be created to sort out conflicts and gaps in agency jurisdiction; to develop methodologies for risk assessment; to coordinate and develop a research program to support rational, regulatory decisionmaking; and to coordinate and maximize the limited scientific expertise available in the federal government.

Shortly after the hearing, the lack of scientific consensus among the different disciplines was illustrated by the willingness of eight or nine environmental scientists to file suit in court to attempt to obstruct the ability of molecular biologists to continue their research outside of laboratory containment. Many professional ecologists do not yet share the confidence of molecular biologists that environmental releases are little, if any, cause for concern.

These fears, and those of the molecular biology community that yet another round of what was referred to as sterile debate could occur, are understandable. But in my opinion, the scientific community must recognize and respect the importance of public acceptance of this new science of biotechnology. The way the public perceives this technology can, and almost certainly will, influence the direction and speed of its development through pressures the public can bring to bear on sources of research funding, legislative initiatives, or regulation and consumer support for new products. Unless environmental, health, and ethical questions are addressed in a sensitive, fair, and open fashion, the existing public consensus underpinning financial support and research freedom could erode. Serious consequences for biotechnology, and perhaps for science in general, would follow.

Therefore, the most important thing for the scientific community to do now is to attack the questions of environmental risks wholeheartedly in a coordinated, multidisciplinary way. As other questions are moved to the front burner, the scientific community must also be willing to bring to bear all of its resources in a full, fair, patient effort to address those questions, and to address the public's concerns about them.

Congress has obligations of its own. Congress, during this period, must ensure that the federal statutes are adequate to establish an efficient and comprehensive system that ensures thorough and timely reviews of the products of biotechnology without unnecessary burdens being placed on the scientists and the industry. Congress must ensure that the United States' leadership in international biotechnology is maintained and enhanced. The best way to do that is to have an adequate commitment of resources to basic research and development.

Finally, Congress must make certain that open public debate is maintained and encouraged. To educate the public on the complex and fascinating issues arising from the diverse applications of biotechnology, access to information must be ensured.

A Scientist's Perspective

JOSHUA LEDERBERG

I AM PRESENTING a general overview of the subject of biotechnology. My difficulty is to extract a few salient points.

Cells are the basic architectural constituents of all biological life, including human beings. The important point is that there is a vast variety of cells. Yet the biochemical basis of all of these cells is the same. This is known as the unity of biochemistry.

Curiously in science, sometimes more is known about a detailed biochemical process than about the organization of chemicals into the structures found in cells. It is remarkable that the accurate identification of the chromosome set in the human was not known until 1955. And yet at that time, scientists were already presuming that advances would occur in research in human development and in genetics. Those hopes came because the structure of DNA—the essential chemical constituent of the chromosome that embodies information—was already known in its physical and chemical detail. Understanding how DNA encodes information dates to 1953, when James D. Watson and Francis Crick published their very famous double helix structural model for DNA.

Human development and genetics

DNA has two functions in the cell. One is to replicate itself faithfully. In replication, the problems are (1) transmission of information from generation to generation and (2) how to ensure that every cell in the body has an appropriate quota of genetic information.

DNA's second function is to influence the structure and character of the cell and the organism. This is done through the medium of another form of nucleic acid called ribonucleic acid (RNA). RNA acts as the messengers of the blueprints of the cell that is present in DNA. This process of selecting parts of the DNA blueprint and putting them into RNA is called transcription. The RNA messengers then move to a structure called the ribosome, where they direct the process of protein synthesis. This process is called translation. The type and function of proteins manufactured on ribosomes provide the unique characterization of any

19

cell. In short, DNA and RNA form a coding mechanism. The DNA is transcribed into an RNA copy, and the information in the RNA then directs the assembly of the amino acids into protein on the ribosome.

Proteins are chemically composed of twenty different amino acids. Proteins differ in the number of amino acids and their order in the protein chain. Each of the amino acids has a very distinctive molecular form. Consequently, after the protein chain is released from the ribosome, it has a built-in propensity to fold up into a very specific, three-dimensional shape. The linear sequence of information, which in itself is a reflection of the linear sequence of information in the RNA, then results in objects that have well-defined shapes and well-defined distributions of specific amino acids. Some of the amino acids will have charges on them; some will repel water, some will attract water; and the shapes themselves will permit attachment to external substances.

The relationship of DNA structure to the structure of proteins is reasonably well understood. Somewhat less is known about the details of how and why proteins fold up, but that they do fold into very well-defined and predetermined kinds of three-dimensional conformations is apparent. When they do so, proteins can perform biological functions. If the proteins attach to one another, they become structural elements like skin or collagen, (for example, hair). If they have chemical specificities, they can function as enzymes that catalyze metabolic reactions. By virtue of their very specific shapes, they can attach to specific molecules in the environment and function as antibodies; or grab onto oxygen and transport it throughout the body; or grab onto cholesterol and transport that through the body, and so on and so forth. These relationships concerning the transfer of DNA information to protein structure are the underpinnings of biotechnology. One can take advantage of this knowledge for further analysis of how cells work and how they produce various products.

A gene can be thought of as the segment of DNA that is responsible for the characterization of some particular protein. An average protein is a chain of one hundred amino acids. Knowing this, one can calculate that, in principle, there can be about 10 million genes in the human organism. To a rough approximation, using our alphabet to match the genetic alphabet, a set or a dozen sets of the Encyclopedia Britannica would be required in order to inscribe that much information. Therefore, if one is to understand the complexity of the human organism, one is going to have to unravel the identities of at least a hundred thousand different gene products. And then the fun begins. Each one of those gene products is worth a chapter, if not volumes, of further investigation. This provides a philosophical perspective that is one of the most important contributions of molecular biology. Human nature is a mechanism of such complexity that it is necessary to be very humble, indeed, about the ability to even understand small parts. Today there is only a glimmer of 1 percent of the knowledge of what the protein constituents of the human body do. Of the thousands of proteins inferred to be present, only a few have been isolated and definitely characterized. In large measure, these are known because of the power of the new tools of biotechnology. Today, there would not be materials like interferon or interleukin-2 if it were not for the intervention of biotechnology as a means of production.

From science to technology

What about biotechnology? In the early 1970s, besides the fundamental understanding of the structure of DNA, a set of tools for handling DNA was developed and allowed science to move into technology. The contributions of many investigators provided the tools to allow the cleavage of DNA at certain selected places in the DNA sequence. These tools are enzymes that are called restriction endonucleases. They function like a search routine in a word processor. The enzymes generate pieces of DNA, whose ends are of a specific nucleotide sequence, and that will form "complementary" pairs with other pieces of DNA generated by the same enzyme. The unity of biochemistry shows that the same rules of DNA structure are shared by bacteria, plants, yeast, algae, other animals, mammals, insects, and so on. So, by using restriction enzymes, a piece of DNA can be removed from one source of DNA and inserted into another.

Other enzymes, called ligases, seal up the chemical bond which is formed when two pieces of DNA form complementary pairs. The final result is that the original DNA, and a piece of DNA that was cut from another source, are joined together. This new, chimeric DNA can then be taken up by bacteria. These bacteria can now be fooled into allowing the indefinite promulgation of foreign DNA. Of course, there are tricks about getting the bacterium to also perform the tasks of transcription and translation, which are needed to get a protein product.

That is the technical base of the recombinant DNA piece of biotechnology. It is important to remember what is easy and what is difficult. It is easy is to take DNA from any source and manipulate it so that in a population of 100 billion bacteria, each bacterium will have one each of the various stretches of DNA that were in the DNA source. This is a totally random process. This is relatively easy. What is more difficult is to first pick out that one bacterium that has picked up the particular DNA wanted. The second difficult task is to get that bacterium to produce the protein wanted. Third, and hardest of all, is to find something really useful to do with the product that has been made.

The discussion to this point has focused on recombinant DNA. But that is not all of biotechnology. Biotechnology has a long history that goes back to the primitive selection of plants for crops. The largest part of the world's food supply is still derived from the choices that our neolithic ancestors made seven, eight, nine thousand years ago. No really important new crops to date have been invented since that time.

Our staples are still rice and wheat. There have been geographic discoveries: the discovery of the New World brought the Irish potato to Ireland from Peru, the tomato from Mexico, and a wide variety of others that have been of indigenous origin. Our ancestors were uncanny in their ability to select and develop plant resources for that purpose.

Much the same has happened in the domestication of animals. The cat, the dog, the cow, the horse, and the goat, have been subjected to extensive, although informal and not scientifically sophisticated, patterns of breeding to achieve specific purposes. The current advances are part of a continuing progressive understanding, and there are many other technologies that are involved in biotechnology.

There is one technology about which there is some misunderstanding. The term genetic therapy is misleading. The current objective of the introduction of genetic information is not at all the alteration of germinal information (which dictates the transmission of characteristics to an offspring), but rather the modification of cells in the body of the individual. In this respect, genetic therapy is not very different from vaccination. For example, with live polio virus vaccination, one introduces genetic information from a foreign source into humans in an attempt to modify the behavior with a desired end. In this case, the desired end is the production of antibodies to polio virus. It is very important that already sensitive issues are not confounded by failing to make important distinctions. Germ cell alteration is something that would deserve the most critical attention.

I was asked to say a few words about what the issues are. I am a little loathe to do so, because I am an interested party. I cannot pretend to have a disinterest in the outcome of decisions about the continuation of modern biological science. As a scientist very much involved in laying some of the underpinnings of biotechnology, I have a commitment to engendering more understanding, and I am eager to see positive uses. I am also eager for there not to be any human disasters as a result of this research. I also have a financial interest in these outcomes. It is very important that I am not perceived as a disinterested party.

The consequences of biotechnology

What are the issues? One very important aspect is to enhance the scientific quality of biomedical research. Biotechnology is framed much too narrowly. The glamour of recombinant DNA has made many forget the many steps requiring hard work in the development of pharmaceutical products. After learning how to produce a product, it is hard to figure out what to do with it. The testing, validation, and discovery of a drug's side effects includes many more disciplines than recombinant DNA. This country is still not doing a very good job in this area. The laboratories of molecular biology are by and large not in sufficiently good contact with their clinical colleagues for the development of those applications of molecular biology research.

I think it is of the utmost importance that biotechnology be directed to the most important human ends. One important human end is the application of molecular genetics to the problems of parasitic disease. Malaria is the world's most important disease, and there are very significant, exciting, provocative ways in which to attack that by using the most advanced of our present technologies. However, currently, it is very difficult to find support for research in this area, from either federal or commercial sources. In agriculture, the situation is similar. There is little motivation for trying to do what would be of the greatest importance in terms of global welfare.

Opportunities exist for applications of biotechnology that may lead to a better understanding of environmental toxicity. Perhaps this country can establish a rational basis for decisions about environmental "clean-up." These priorities must be founded on scientific knowledge of how environmental chemicals relate to genetic structures.

Social consequence of success in this new field must be anticipated. Realities are sliding right by that have enormous implications for the future. The success of programs in biomedical investigation will have the most important consequences. Biomedical research can contribute to the alleviation of disease. The conquest of heart disease and of cancer is already wreaking a change in our demographic structure, in the relationship of old to young, and in the interval of progressive disability. Those are the important consequences of biomedical advance. Biotechnology cannot be isolated from the whole framework of biomedical application. The same is true for agriculture. The success of programs in enhancing the efficiency of food production key to the economies of the developed world is very likely to cause major disruption in world agricultural markets that must be thought about very seriously. Otherwise, the United States may discover that it has the technology and the land, that it can produce all the world's food, and nobody else can afford to do it because others cannot compete with this country. What a terrible situation that would be in a global economy. Yet society seems to be heading there like an express train.

Biotechnology: What Are the Problems beyond Regulation?

JOHN D. DINGELL

THE TECHNOLOGY that is creating a biological revolution is in for a new round of intense congressional scrutiny. When I became aware of a set of developments in September 1983, I wrote to the director of the National Institutes of Health (NIH). I noted the two changes that caused my concern and that have brought the House Energy and Commerce Committee back to looking at biotechnology.

First, the NIH was being asked to make decisions about releasing genetically engineered organisms. The process created by the National Institutes of Health Recombinant DNA Advisory Committee, which was designed to make decisions about containing dangerous organisms in laboratories, was being altered to review and to approve intentional releases into the environment. This change indicated that stress was being imposed upon the NIH system, which it perhaps could not meet.

Second, the users of genetic engineering were no longer the research laboratories and the universities, but, increasingly, commercial entities contemplating industrial-scale processes. The NIH had no way to ensure compliance with its decisions. Its program was voluntary.

In a meeting with James Wyngaarden, director of the NIH, I asked him to make the recognized expertise of the NIH in genetic engineering available to the committee to design a workable regulatory program to protect the public health and environment. I appreciate the help we have received from Dr. Wyngaarden and his colleagues. The committee is moving forward.

Within months, the administration began its own review of the regulation of biotechnology at the cabinet council level. The council has been inquiring about the adequacy of current laws and how programs can be altered and coordinated to produce effective regulation of biotechnology.

It is important to recognize that Congress and the executive branch approach their reviews from different perspectives. The administration must begin working within the authority it has.

25

Its job is to adapt the administration of programs to meet new challenges as best it can.

New
developments

Congress is aware that the existing legislation was not drafted either to promote the development of biotechnology or to protect against its associated risks. Congress was not anticipating this new technology when it enacted the laws to deal with toxic chemicals, foods and drugs, pesticides, and the breeding and selection of plants and animals. Even the most appropriate and intelligent administration of current programs may not suffice. Specific statutory amendments to fix discrete problems or a new and comprehensive approach to protecting the public from the risks of the biological revolution may be needed.

The Oversight and Investigations Subcommittee of the House Energy and Commerce Committee began an intensive review of the scientific and commercial development of biotechnology in May 1984. The inquiry is focused on the role of the federal government in all of the subcommittee's areas of jurisdiction. The most urgent concern is the apparent inadequacy of the base of scientific knowledge used by the federal agencies to formulate judgments about new developments.

I intend to preside over a thorough review of the adequacy of all of the applicable laws, the process by which the executive branch determines how to interpret and to apply the current authority, and the implementation of the programs.

The first hearing was very instructive to me. The administration's witnesses were responsive and constructive. Their answers to the subcommittee's questions were far more revealing than their formal statements or the carefully written notice that appeared in the *Federal Register* on December 31, 1984. The witnesses all agreed that current laws, regulations, and programs may be flawed and require revision. There was certainly no unqualified assertion that everything could work unchanged. They also agreed that additional research was needed to reduce the scientific uncertainty in the regulation of biotechnology, particularly intentional releases of genetically engineered organisms. It seems likely that any legislation proposed by this committee will authorize a range of needed research initiatives.

When the committee looked at regulation to protect the public health and environment, the first thing discovered was the pressing need for research. New questions, however, are brought to the committee's attention almost daily. Some people have focused on regulation because of a legitimate concern about the dangers of genetically engineered organisms. Others are convinced that regulation is the only role for government, as they believe all research and development should be left to the private sector.

I am certain that society faces real dangers from the use of biotechnology; but there are also serious human and economic consequences from choosing not to make use of the technology. This, too, will be the subject of the committee's inquiry. Today, I have very few answers, but let me lay out eight questions that demand answers.

First, will the industrial domination of biotechnology research imperil basic research in the future? Two historical observations are essential to understanding the problems society may face. The critical discoveries in genetic engineering emerged from basic research, from scientists trying to understand how living organisms work. No one was looking for a commercial breakthrough. In addition, the basic research was funded almost exclusively by the U.S. government, specifically the National Institutes of Health and the National Science Foundation. This early and wise public investment predated commercial interest. But by 1980, industry was able to adopt and apply this scientific legacy toward improving its products or making entirely new ones.

Two more recent developments prompt me to worry about the whole future of basic research. There were some immediate and important commercial opportunities offered by genetic engineering. These attracted a few researchers into industry, both by starting new firms and joining old ones. It looked as if industry was eager to support academic biotechnology research. At the same time in history, the Reagan administration began to cut back on the federal nonmilitary research budget. The National Institutes of Health, which funded most of the molecular biology, ceased to grow. Universities were strapped, and researchers looked for more promising futures.

The danger, as I see it, is overreacting. One reaction is to treat the commercial interest in molecular biology as dominant and cede responsibility for all future research funding to industry. Then cuts in federal biomedical research funding may erode the scientific resources in universities that have done the basic research, the training, and provided most of the stimulation that has led the brightest students to choose careers in science.

The public interest

Will a radical change in the university climate created by commercial objectives and industrial funding mean that U.S. universities can never again initiate a scientific revolution?

- My second question is, will the development strategies of the commercial interests be sufficiently broad to serve fully the public interest? It is possible to conceive of dozens of uses for biotechnology that have little commercial value but obvious social value. The example that comes to mind most quickly is the malaria vaccine. Over 150 million people get malaria each year, but they are among the poorest people in the world. What commercial incentive exists to invest development money if the potential consumers have no buying power? Has this dilemma already slowed the development of malaria vaccine?

Local production of protein with single cellular organisms may solve the food problems of the world, but such a revolution is in conflict with conventional agriculture. Can agribusiness encourage a technology that may undermine its prosperity? And the same chemical companies that could do the genetic engineering for protein production have a lucrative pesticide business to protect.

It seems appropriate to encourage the private sector to develop those products that are marketable. But where the products of biotechnology can make such qualitative contributions without direct return on private investment, may it not be necessary for the government to set policy and provide funding?

• My third question is, will biotechnology constitute a major escalation of the potential for biological warfare and terrorism? Simplistic assertions that genetic engineering is harmless are always refuted by the obvious potential for use in germ warfare. The ability to produce toxins in organisms different from the original microbe that produces the toxin enhances the ability to change where and how pathogens will grow. Thus new and more dangerous weapons are possible.

Are the current treaties sufficient to protect the United States? If the United States is doing research on vaccines and defense against biological warfare, are the Russians doing the same? And developing vaccines to protect one's own soldiers and population is not very different from the research that would be needed to develop the weapons themselves.

Can the public be assured that the new containment facility being built in Utah is not the first step in a new round of biological armaments? Is there any reason to believe that genetic engineering of biological weapons is beyond the reach of less technologically sophisticated terrorists?

Fourth, will public misunderstanding of human genetics and biotechnology mean that ghosts of the Scopes trial will haunt each new discovery and every new therapy? I hear a variety of views about the concept of species. Scientists emphasize the

inevitable mutability of all life forms while others dwell
sanctity of those existing at this moment in evolution. It is
that this talk should occur just as molecular genetics is resha ...g
the whole concept of the species. Can we keep an open mind
long enough to develop a good scientific understanding of genetics
and disease, and how we can prevent and cure disease genetically?
Or will the same forces who oppose research on animals reject
all research on human genetics?

One of the issues that must be confronted is inherent in the
course of research and understanding about human genetics. It
will be possible to detect human genetic defects—even in unborn
fetuses—long before we can hope to correct the genetic problem.
Thus society is entering a limited period—until treatment catches
up with diagnosis—in which abortions will be one approach to
avoiding a genetically diseased child. Even then, what can be
diagnosed is limited compared with the full range of possible
genetic defects. Will society shut down the research that may lead
to valuable treatment because in the short run it seems to encourage
abortion?

There may be other difficulties associated with early genetic
screening and diagnosis. Individuals who are genetically suscep-
tible to certain diseases can be protected—by exclusion—from
situations that are particularly hazardous to them. Will this mean
that some will suffer inappropriate discrimination as well? Will
there be job losses where job transfer would suffice? Or, even
worse, will some be locked out of broad sectors of employment
based on a record indicating a specific genetic susceptibility to a
specific chemical?

In fact, the fundamental basis of our egalitarian attitudes toward
individuals could erode. As the genetic makeup of an individual
becomes fully described, one could become less and less likely to
treat everyone as having equal potential and deserving equal
opportunities. Such major changes in attitude might result from
the technology that can detect and describe minute changes in
genes.

A fifth question is, can the public debate about genetic engineering and biotechnology be improved? I hope Congress can
open the debate and encourage further public understanding and
participation. There is a real danger that a new science can create
radical change before the public is conversant with the issues and
prepared to participate in the debate. In fact, there is probably
greater danger from creating an exclusive policymaking process
than from any direct consequence of genetic engineering. Not

having all the answers now is not a fault, but decisionmakers will be guilty of serious negligence if they fail to ask questions about the opportunities and consequences of genetic engineering and biotechnology. And decisionmakers will lose the public's trust if they fail to create a process that the public can understand and in which it can participate.

Discussion about intentional release to the environment of genetically engineered organisms now includes scientists, industrial firms, and government agencies, but each has narrow concerns and interests. The public interest community that is usually well informed on environmental issues has been largely silent on genetic engineering. Is it kept at a distance by the complex science, or overwhelmed by the industry's swift emergence?

So far, the mainstream environmental organizations have left center stage to Jeremy Rifkin, a clever advocate with an apocalyptic view of scientific progress. Maybe the environmentalists cannot respond to the challenge of biotechnology until there has been a disaster, but I believe they can make a useful contribution to this early phase of the debate.

A sixth question is, if society lacks the means to prevent or cope with accidents like the release of methylisocyanate in Bhopal, India, are there any adequate preparations to deal with emergencies arising in the biotechnology industry? Accidental releases of genetically engineered organisms to the environment are a continuing potential problem.

I was pleased to learn that the European Economic Community is planning to expand the Seveso Convention—an agreement that all member states will plan and prepare for toxic chemical emergencies. The revision, due in 1986, will include coverage of biological accidents as well as chemical spills.

Seventh, will the threat of tort liability owing to unforeseen consequences of the technology conspire to discourage established and conservative firms from entering the field, leaving the action to less risk-adverse buccaneers? In a field that requires little capital and only a few talented scientists, I am concerned about the small firm that wants to make a financial killing quickly. They have little to lose for themselves and a lot to risk for everyone else.

The nuclear industry has special protection under the law. Asbestos makers would like to be pardoned for the human damage they have done. And vaccine manufacturers are clamoring for special protection against injuries caused by their vaccines. Will there be a similar problem in biotechnology?

And will the biotechnology industry move abroad if there is

the chance that other countries or their courts will be more lenient? How Union Carbide fares in India may be critical.

My final question is, will new interpretations and extension of patent law to life forms serve the public interest? Are further changes needed? Patents seem to remove some of the industrial secrecy that makes it difficult for scientists to work in an industrial environment. But if university scientists are trying to get rich by patenting their discoveries, are we reducing collegial communication to the detriment of intellectual advances for the whole field of molecular biology? And are we limiting the segment of society that will benefit from the new discoveries?

These are just a few of the questions that must be asked about biotechnology. The regulatory questions cannot be stopped because society has as much to lose from failing to use every opportunity offered by the technology as by failing to avoid the hazards. This committee intends to spend this Congress in diligently reviewing biotechnology and creating legislation to correct the important problems uncovered.

Basic Science: A Gift from the Biotechnology Industry

LEWIS THOMAS

THE SCIENTIFIC advances that underlie most of today's biotechnology and make it possible to put biological processes to profitable use on an industrial scale are chiefly the new disciplines of molecular genetics and cell biology. Short strings of DNA meticulously separated from the rest of the cells' genome can now be isolated in pure form. These are then inserted into other organisms that become factories for the production of gene products.

The capacity of biological science to do this is surely one of the wonders of modern technology and provides high hopes for the future. Yet the hopes are for more than the production of useful products for the marketplace. These to be sure are very important and may well revolutionize some aspects of the practice of medicine and agriculture, and perhaps new energy sources and disposal of waste materials.

It is now possible to ask questions about living organisms and living processes that were simply inconceivable ten or fifteen years ago. The answers may at first seem short, clear, and unequivocal, but will then quickly be recognized as having some strangeness of their own. They will raise new, more puzzling questions, and that is the way science goes when the going is real good.

Pure biomedical science has never before possessed such power to raise questions with strange answers. When I was a junior researcher beginning a career, it was taken for granted that most of the really big questions of the working of cells, or about the immune system, or about the brain, and certainly about most human disease mechanisms, including cancer, were simply unapproachable. The greatest part of nature was regarded as a permanent mystery, forever beyond human reach. Now it is possible to do research on almost any problem, even on the operation of the human brain, and to expect new information to come in steadily in the decades ahead. We may not necessarily gain an understanding of the human mind, of course—this may elude our grasp forever—but at least we can begin to get on with studying its main source. As for cancer, it has not yet been solved, but there is lively consensus among the youngest and brightest

32

investigators that it now has the look of a potentially solvable problem, and this is something quite new.

Pure biomedical research has gotten so mixed up with product-oriented research that it is becoming difficult to tell these two enterprises apart. The industrial laboratories that are pressing for useful products and new ways to the genetic engineering of such products, are under their own kind of pressure for results, but nobody, I think, expects or is any longer pressing for quick results. The investments in these laboratories are to be long-term investments, longer indeed than what has been customary in the past for R&D in other kinds of industry.

Meanwhile, the same laboratories are running into new kinds of information almost every day, and a lot of it demands to be followed up even when it seems unrelated to the matter at hand. This happens because the information, as it comes in, is surprising and strange and new.

Part of the work now going on in the industry laboratories is becoming similar to, and closely connected to, the kind of research one expects to encounter in the laboratories of research universities. It is partly because of this that the contractual agreements now being worked out between the world of corporate biotechnology and certain university laboratories are turning out to be equitable and agreeable to all the investigators involved. They are all working on the same sorts of problems.

Classifying scientific research

It used to be a simple matter to classify the major types of scientific endeavor. There were only two—basic research and applied research. Each possessed such conspicuous and sharply restricted features that there was no problem in distinguishing one from the other. Basic science was carried out in a certain style, for a certain purpose, and it needed a particular kind of support over an indefinite, unspecified period of time. Applied science had a quite different purpose. It was performed in an altogether different style, and when it was done well, it had to meet hard deadlines.

In the last few years, the distinctions have turned fuzzy, and it is a puzzle now to decide whether this or that line of research should be labeled as basic or applied. The new ambiguity entails some new risks for the national science policy, since the old criteria had the great advantage of allowing the system to set quite different standards for approval, for funding, and for organization of the research, and most important of all, for agreeing in advance on the expectations.

Here is the way it used to be. Applied science, as the term suggests, consisted of making use of an array of solid, established bits of information in order to produce something useful and usable. Usually, but not necessarily, this was marketable as a product. Two elements were regarded as essential aspects of the process: feasibility and time.

To begin a venture in applied research, it was considered necessary to be able to predict with a high degree of certainty that the available facts at hand pointed in a certain direction toward a certain target. The central question confronting investigators was how to reach the target, with the highest efficiency, and within the shortest possible time.

Given enough certainty about the outcome, the lines of research were drawn with as much exactitude and rigor as possible. Charts illustrating the proposed flow of events with boxes and arrows arranged along a calendar of future dates were useful for budgeting the cost of the operation over time. Individual investigators were assigned specific tasks to be accomplished, and all parties had to agree in advance on the allocation of their specific functions. The workers behaved after the fashion of teams. Frequently, since applied science involved competition among various groups aiming at the same target, intricately coordinated teamwork was an indispensable ingredient for success.

When it worked, as it has from time to time over many decades, the collective reaction on the part of the investigators was a shared sense of satisfaction that things turned out as they should have turned out. The emergence of the polio vaccine under the leadership of Jonas Salk and Thomas Francis and their colleagues was an elegant example of applied science in biomedical research.

When a good idea in applied research failed to work, when the product was found not to be reachable, and when the basic fact on which the whole effort was based turned out not to lead as predicted, the collective reaction was one of surprise and dismay.

Basic research was something else. Here the ambition of the investigators was not for any product other than comprehension. The questions started with, "What if?" and the hypotheses to be tested by experimentation were always guesses. There were imaginary stories about a mechanism in nature, which might or might not turn out to be true stories, and usually they were not, not more than perhaps one in a hundred times.

The great surprise sometimes came when an investigator discovered that he had been right in his guess. Once in a while, if on a very lucky streak, the first reaction to an experimental result was dismay, but that quickly turned into a combination of surprise and delight, because the problem had turned out to be different. The more interesting problem allowed a totally new set of guesses, leading in a different direction and maybe down a garden path.

The test of a good investigator was his or her capacity to tell the difference between a garden path and a blind alley. The research went on in an atmosphere of high uncertainty. Investigators and their colleagues changed their minds whenever they wanted to, and there was no such thing as time. Schedules were laid out for the work, but in the expectation that they were likely to be changed at any moment.

The moment of astonishment, which was the real reward in basic research, came in the form of an epiphany, and this would begin in one of several different ways. One initial reaction, and I think the most common one, was for investigators to say to themselves, or to nearby colleagues, something has gone wrong—I am right. More often than not, the first sign that a piece of basic research is going to turn out nicely is a sense of high comedy. Whenever a small item of truth begins to emerge in nature, it often makes an appearance looking like something extremely funny, something to be laughed at. Only later, it becomes something to be looked at in deadly earnest.

For a long time in this country, the two biomedical science communities engaged in applied and basic research, viewed themselves as quite separate from each other—intellectually unconnected, and up to entirely different kinds of occupations. One was based largely in the pharmaceutical and chemical industries, and a few in government laboratories; the other lived almost exclusively in the country's universities.

New relationships between industry and academe

Whatever relationship did exist was largely ceremonial, more or less adversarial. People doing applied research thought of themselves as practical, hard-working types doing the Lord's work. They viewed the university scientists as a dreamy, unworldly, ivory tower lot, useful for bits of information that could be put to use from time to time, but distinguished mainly for the gift of wasting time and money, and having too much fun. The basic researchers thought of themselves as the source of the only true knowledge, as pure scientists, uncontaminated by any smell of the marketplace, and they regarded industrial researchers as money-grubbing day laborers, only good at swiping information.

All that has changed, in just the last few years, and on balance, all for the better. The two communities have begun to draw together, and they have discovered to the surprise of some that neither they as persons nor their everyday work is all that different. The relationship will doubtless become even closer in the years ahead, particularly within the fields of biomedical research. This is partly because the industry is now more aware than ever of its dependence on basic research for whatever new products it will have for the decades ahead, and partly because the university laboratories, in their avarice, can now begin to look to industry as a possible source of funds.

The latter is a relatively new phenomenon in biomedical science, and it needs the most thoughtful and cautious planning for the long term for the new university-industry connection to be as mutually profitable as it should be. Up to now, the relationship has been developing rapidly, but with the very encouraging signs of good taste and even elegance on both sides. Indeed, it seems to me that the major universities and the major industries that have been launching partnership arrangements have displayed a remarkable degree of enlightened sensitivity to academic concerns, and I am quite optimistic for the turn of events in the near future.

Right now, the connections look eminently workable. The corporation, for example, may perceive that a department or a group of investigators within a department is doing basic research on problems related to the industry's own commercial interests. It may agree to invest a certain amount of money in the group over a substantial period, maybe five or maybe as long as ten years—I hope someday even longer. The academic researchers are not expected to change what they are doing, nor even encouraged to take on new lines of research for the company's benefit. The expected return is early access to the information generated by the university laboratory, so that the corporation can decide whether that information can be turned to practical applications.

In some instances, the questions of confidentiality and secrecy have been faced directly, and some university laboratories have even agreed to delay publication for varying periods of time, while the industrial partner has time to move for patenting or licensing. In another arrangement the companies have only asked for the benefit of the first look at the results, without imposing any restraint or delay in publications. And for still others, the industry reserves the right to purchase certain products—monoclonal antibodies, for example—being made in the academic laboratories for its own interest. In return for these arrangements, the laboratory receives financial support for its more general research programs.

Meanwhile, other institutional changes have been taking place on both the university and industry sides, designed to improve their relationship in other ways. One remarkable phenomenon has been the voluntary transfer of a number of distinguished university scientists out of academia and directly into executive posts in the industrial sciences. As a natural outcome of this, a significant number of very bright, young investigators at the postdoctoral level now also plan to follow their seniors into industrial research. At a few institutions, opportunities have been created for traffic back and forth between the university and industry, on the part of the youngest researchers on both sides.

All of this sounds good, and it ought to augur well for the future. Everyone or nearly everyone seems to agree that the long divorce between the academic and industrial worlds of science has placed this country at a disadvantage in the competition for technological advancement against, say, Europe and Japan. An improvement in coherent collaboration between the two enterprises can only improve the United States' competitive position in the short term.

Research in the long term

It is the long term that is beginning to worry me now. I can see lots of practical advantages to be gained by both sides by a close, amiable, symbiotic relationship between industry and the universities, especially at a time when the federal government's investment in basic science is on a flat line, or a down-sloping line. It is a good way to keep the basic research laboratories in operation, even to modestly expand operation. I have no doubt that some of the research being supported will turn out to be useful and profitable for many of the companies.

Surely the kinds of investment now being made are going to have the effect of stabilizing the university laboratories, and especially their junior personnel. The increasing instability of university science in the last few years has been badly damaging to the morale, and therefore to the recruitment of the youngest generation of American biomedical scientists. I am, therefore, completely in favor of the new partnership arrangements, and I hope we are going to see more in the way of institutional experiments.

My anxiety over the long term concerns the kinds of science that scientists may find themselves not doing. If, as I think it may, the new working relationships between academia and industry are a spectacular success in ferreting out truth about basic mechanisms in nature, and at the same time, achieve practical technological advances, some questions will inevitably slip away before they are asked. Any young scientist placed in this setting is likely to wonder whether his research is going to turn out to be one of the ultimate successes, the useful and usable ones. Too many of the youngest and brightest people now working on the most profound problems in molecular genetics and cellular immunology are, I think, already spending too much of their time hankering to have their particular line of research explode into a product for patenting.

Under today's circumstances, I do not see how this attitude can be avoided, and I have to say I do not see anything wrong with it for the individual scientist. But my dismay would come if every young scientist developed the same deep wish for his science, for this would surely begin to have sooner or later a devastating impact on the range of scientific problems to be selected for exploration. At the same time it would begin to affect disastrously the merit system for the selection and advancement of academic scientists up through the ranks.

One outcome to worry about especially concerns the uncertainty and the lack of time constraints that should characterize true, basic research. If you are a young investigator in the laboratory receiving generous corporate support for research, you would surely see your job as finding items of a fundamental nature that could then be put to use. You would want to do this as quickly as possible. Accordingly, you might select problems with this future and stay away from other sorts of puzzles, even ones about which you might be deeply curious. If this begins to happen, it is not going to work. Virtually every useful advance in medical or biological technology has had its origin in earlier basic research. I can think of very few occasions when it could have been foreseen that a particular piece of fundamental research was going to lead to something useful. The two most promising technologies in biology today would seem to me to be recombinant DNA and monoclonal antibodies. They had their beginnings in experiments done for other reasons, out of pure curiosity, and not because any of the people involved had anything remotely resembling a product on their minds.

Still, a system of research support involving industrial science is an improvement over what we have had in recent years. I regard the National Institutes of Health (NIH) as the single greatest and most enlightened social invention of modern times in the world. I view the NIH as absolutely indispensable for the future of biomedical science and medicine. Yet there is an important role to be played as well by the private sector. With a shortage of NIH funds for basic research, and the increasing competitiveness for grants and the immensity of the bureaucratic machine required for the NIH mission, there has emerged a new tendency for grants to be awarded on shorter and shorter time bases, and for projects that look more and more like sure-fire bets.

The tendency is for young investigators to take up problems that look as though a publishable answer can be attained with certainty within the next twelve months. In this time, the data can be used in the application for grant renewal. Few grants run for more than two or three years. Grant applications have to be written at enormous length, and in exquisite detail to persuade the study section that the project is going to turn out exactly as predicted, which means that a lot of safe and sound projects are becoming the mode.

Relevance has become the code word for projects that fit neatly into the current paradigm. This means that less research is being launched on long shots or outright gambles, and even less research on that very life blood of science, the pure hunch.

Another thing is going wrong. It used to be that grant applications were relatively brief accounts of the investigator's ideas, laying out in general terms the future direction planned for the work, and in particular, the kinds of questions that the investigator had on his mind. It was the quality and originality of these ideas that made the difference between acceptance and rejection.

Nowadays, the applications have become great, long documents as detailed and as complicated as a laboratory notebook, stipulating every single technique for every single experiment, and laying out the whole run of experiments seriatim, step by step for the next two years, at least. Not at all as if what is intended is basic research, where the changing of minds and direction is taken for granted as essential steps in successful research; more as if what is being proposed is a kind of applied science project. And this is the wrong way to plan basic research, but it would not be such a bad thing if it were taken as sort of a legal fiction, to be adhered to or not, depending on how the laboratories' affairs progressed. The trouble now is that these ponderous documents are indeed being taken seriously. Worst of all, they are taken seriously by the young investigators who wrote them.

This fundamental mistake uses the method and approach of applied science for planning and executing basic research. This new delusionary concept, the adherence to long, intricately detailed protocols may turn out to be the deadest of all dead ends on the face of basic science.

So in the present circumstance, other sources, modest ones, of research funding should be welcome, and may be necessary, especially if the support can be used at least to stabilize the salaries of young investigators through the early years of their careers. Hence, my enthusiasm for the new phenomenon, the university and industry collaboration. But I fervently hope that those in charge of the enterprise, and both the academic and corporate ends, will do whatever they can to ensure that the research that they sponsor is an inquiry based on ungovernable, insatiable curiosity, carried out because the problems are in themselves irresistible, and rewarded by the pure fun of doing the work.

It is often remarked by those who worry most about the hazards of modern technology, that anything that can be done will be done. In biology, I suspect that the aphorism needs editing to read, in biology anything that can be done, nature has already done, probably over and over.

Not that there are no dangers. Anyone here can think of foolish, feckless experiments that should never be undertaken, and some sort of regulation is needed, I suppose, to monitor the system and prevent foolishness. But I would be deeply worried if it were to be judged that in general, experiments in gene transfer should be inhibited on the grounds of sin. I worry, of course, because of the restraint of what looks like an elegant technology for making useful products, but I would worry very much more for the future of my own field, medicine.

The prospects for biological science, learning sometime before long how nature really works, are beginning to look very bright indeed. It is this deep level of comprehension that medicine is going to need for coping with most of the unsolved diseases now on society's agenda.

Regulation in Biotechnology

JAMES J. FLORIO

SOCIETY IS at a crossroad with respect to the difficult question of the safety features to be or not be built into the rapidly expanding industry of biotechnology. It is possible to approach the issues raised by potential governmental involvement with a strong and paradoxical mixture of hopeful idealism and discouraged cynicism.

There is hope because biotechnology as a commercial venture now stands at the same threshold that was passed long ago by many other successful industries. More than a decade of intense research has developed several products of potentially enormous implication for the improvement of the quality of life. Almost daily, one reads of genetically engineered substances that could solve some of the most intractable problems, products that could neutralize millions of tons of hazardous waste oil currently choking the environment, or that could prevent plants from being destroyed by freezing temperatures, thus increasing technology's capacity to feed millions of people around the world, many of whom suffer from the threat of famine.

At the threshold

Products stand at the brink of commercial development and will soon begin to be manufactured in large quantities. The explosion of laboratory and university research projects into commercial ventures is just beginning, creating the opportunity to address the environment and the human health implications of such developments. Society is confronted with a new industrial revolution and with the chance to correct past mistakes. Government can coordinate the need for protective health and environment with the needs of fledgling and innovative industry.

Society hopes to be wise enough to avoid situations like DDT, Three Mile Island, Love Canal, and Bhopal.

Congress intends to protect the workers who make new products from the devastation of occupational diseases like asbestosis and mesothelioma and to do all that is necessary without hobbling American industry in needless layers of suffocating red

41

tape. Congress will refuse to adopt any knee-jerk regulatory programs that defeat American industry's ability to compete in the world markets. The United States must compete in the world markets.

Although I share the commitment to optimism represented by this conference, I have to describe my discouraged cynicism. Many champions of this industry sincerely believe that the environmental and the human health risks posed by its products are dwarfed by the potential social benefits that they can confer. As has happened so many times in earlier periods of rapid change, a great amount of time has been spent debating the relative safety of new applications of biotechnology and attempting to quantify the risk of catastrophe.

The Cassandras talk darkly of Andromeda strains, of developments that could change the ecology of the earth in a relatively short period of time. The Babbitts scoff at that gloom, dismissing past mistakes as minor laboratory accidents, explaining about the implications of thwarting innovation and suffocating this fledgling industry in an irrational overreaction to extremely remote events. Rational analysis of the science is somewhere between the two extremes. Although it is certainly true that the majority, perhaps even the vast majority, of biotechnological applications are clearly safe, the small but real possibility exists that an unsupervised, incompetent researcher or developer could unleash problems that could pose an unacceptable toll in lost lives and natural resource loss.

Minimizing danger

The question is not whether or how likely such disasters are, but, what can and should be done to minimize the potential threat. Here, history tends to side with both the Cassandras and the Babbitts. Undue preoccupation with risk does stifle innovation and can kill an infant industry. Yet one disaster might spark such a public reaction that the industry would die in adolescence. In recent years, it has become far more fashionable to worry about the death of innovation than about the risk of a crippling disaster. It is the sense of compounded error that gives rise to my cynicism.

Only two years ago, many in this new industry were firmly entrenched in the view that the voluntary program run by the National Institutes of Health Recombinant DNA Advisory Committee (RAC) was completely sufficient as a regulatory surrogate. They brushed aside criticisms of the voluntary and therefore essentially uncontrollable nature of the NIH oversight, even when some of the more boisterous and self-confident members of the industry threatened openly to bolt from even the NIH's gentle structure.

As the history of United States industrial development shows, disputes about the health and safety of the country most often end up in the courts. There, judges, untrained in the scientific and economic nuances of what is at stake, do their best to divide the baby in half. Judge John Sirica recently halted an experiment, which many thought was valid and safe, on legal grounds not anticipated by industry.[1] That produced a change in perspective in many quarters. It becomes clear that without some form of public protection, neither the Cassandras nor the courts will rest.

We therefore have the pronouncements of the White House's Cabinet Council Working Group on Biotechnology, which give the administration's official blessing to the efforts of the Food and Drug Administration, the Environmental Protection Agency, the Occupational Safety and Health Administration, and the Department of Agriculture to apply existing regulatory requirements to emerging commercial ventures in biotechnology.

Federal statutes

The problem with all of this is that it is a sham. And a potentially dangerous one. There is no sign in sight that the Environmental Protection Agency even imagines devoting adequate resources to understanding this new industry. And yet, the mechanisms of one of the most difficult and ponderous federal environmental statutes now on the books—the Toxic Substances Control Act (TSCA)—to regulate traditional chemical products, has been activated allegedly by the flip of a bureaucratic switch for the purpose of regulating biogenetic products.

Consider the current implementation of the TSCA. The Environmental Protection Agency's program for controlling hazardous new chemicals under the act is a fiasco. The agency has never established a meaningful testing program to gather essential health effects data. Its efforts to enforce the minimal requirements of the law are virtually nonexistent. According to a comprehensive study conducted by the Office of Technology Assessment, over half of the premanufacturing notices filed for new chemicals did not

1. A suit was filed against the National Institutes of Health on the grounds that the NIH had failed to comply with the National Environmental Protection Act in adequately assessing the environmental risks of reviewing certain "deliberate release" experiments. *Foundation on Economic Trends, Jeremy Rifkin, Michael W. Fox, Environmental Action Incorporated, and Environmental Task Force* v. *Margaret Heckler, James E. Wyngaarden, and Richard Krause.* Civil Action No. 83–2714 (United States District Court for the District of Columbia, May 16, 1984).

contain any information regarding toxicity. The EPA is therefore placed in the untenable position of reviewing and clearing these new chemicals for production, with little if any idea of their potential threat to human health and the environment.

Once a new chemical has been cleared, it joins the large inventory of sixty thousand existing chemicals. The EPA has taken action to regulate these existing chemicals on only six occasions since the Toxic Substances Control Act was enacted eight years ago. If mistakes are made at the beginning of the new chemical review process, it is highly unlikely that they will ever be corrected.

Concerning EPA enforcement, the EPA has never launched a credible effort to ensure that even those required to file premanufacturing notices actually do so, much less that notices contain the information required under the law. The larger, more reputable firms appear to be complying with these requirements, but little is known of the overall industry compliance rate. These basic enforcement efforts are defeated by the EPA's general lack of resources and the will to implement the law effectively.

What then is the likely result of a rote application of the toxic control act to biogenetics? Responsible companies will desperately attempt to wend their way through the ponderous bureaucratic struggle, eagerly awaiting either nonexistent or overly severe review by the Environmental Protection Agency. At the same time, the cowboy entrepreneurs of a new industry will sidestep the regulatory process, because the EPA has yet to even conceive of an effective policy to enforce the toxic control act for traditional chemicals, much less for exotic new chemicals or exotic new products under biotechnology innovations.

Related to this sad situation is the fact that the EPA's research programs have been decimated. This has occurred just when the EPA's capability to initiate research in ecology should be expanded because of the concerns imposed by biotechnology.

It is significant to note the disbanding of the EPA's Scientific Advisory Committee on ecologic effects of new organisms. This group was studying DNA issues early in this administration. The cabinet council's pronouncement assumes that agencies such as the EPA will be able to exercise real jurisdiction over these initiatives. Yet the government's capabilities are not much more than window dressing. Rather than developing positive new initiatives and approaches to the issues raised by this innovative industry, government depends on old and outmoded regulatory structures that have even failed to deal with the more traditional environmental and health risk questions.

Industry might very well ask, "as long as government stays out from underfoot of this industry, why should we care that agencies like the EPA will undertake the usual wheel spinning in response to an exaggerated perception of an environmental risk? We are not wasting taxpayers' money; we are not wasting industry resources on an abortive effort to stifle legitimate products."

I respond that the public and Congress must be concerned about the scenario of pretended government involvement for four basic reasons. First, even a sham federal program has clear potential to trap the responsible and benefit the irresponsible industry. Second, the pretense of regulation lulls the public into a false sense of security and has the potential to fuel a frightening backlash if a disaster does occur. Third, the lack of an effective program probably will not stop and may accelerate the deferral of decisions about unresolved problems to the federal court system. The ad hoc and uncertain nature of the decisions that would result from this will not give industry the security that it so badly needs if it is going to develop in an orderly way. Fourth, government's decision "to punt" means that we are rolling the dice on the potential for a disaster.

The states are beginning to produce rumblings about independent efforts to regulate biotechnology. The backlash produced by environmental accident in this area would be real and unpleasant. The states may act even without a single national event that galvanizes public attention when they perceive that the federal government is merely going through the motions in this area of regulatory review.

I have no easy solutions. Some review mechanism to distinguish the valid experiments and products from the potentially dangerous ones would be desirable. Those pursuing valid, safe projects would be left in peace. Those running a risk would be carefully supervised. The review mechanism needs the attention of the best scientific minds. Such a mechanism must have the confidence of the public, through some degree of public accountability.

Bureaucratic procedures that become monuments to themselves must be avoided. Striking a balance will take a serious pragmatic commitment of energy, sensitivity, and resources. I emphasize a pragmatic approach, as opposed to an extreme ideological approach that holds on the one hand that government has no role, or alternatively, that government has the total role in dealing with this biotechnology.

The Ninety-ninth Congress will undoubtedly continue to search for the ideal system. I look forward to working with all who have expertise as national policy is formulated.

Research, Commercialization, and the Future

GEORGE B. RATHMANN

IN THE PAST, much about biotechnology was overstated. There was substantial disagreement about what biotechnology promised. There was not much question of the conviction that biotechnology would have enormous impact on society. Different surveys projected a range of sales as a result of the applications of this technology. Some projected $64 billion in sales by the year 2000; others claimed $3 billion, $9 billion, $10 billion, or $13 billion.

There was also significant variability in the projected timing of appearance and size of markets. For example, in the energy area, it was believed that an impact would not occur until well into the twenty-first century. No milestones have been met in the last few years. Although biotechnology may have an impact on dependency upon fossil fuels, the impact is off in the future.

The promise surrounding chemical products was broad and included industrial enzymes, fibers and plastics, specialty chemicals, animal husbandry chemicals, food processing agents, albumen and enzymes and blood expanders, and so on. Many of these chemicals are no longer of high priority, and others have displaced some of the early candidates. What of this promise was delivered?

In January 1980, there was the announcement of the tour de force that led to the cloning of interferon. In 1980, monoclonal antibodies, a product of advanced biotechnology, represented less than 2 percent of the diagnostic products being produced at that time. Today, monoclonal antibodies are a dominant factor in the diagnostic business, providing better, more specific, more sensitive, diagnostic ability.

The use of DNA molecules as hybridization probes has defined a new sensitivity range—the attamolar range—which provides detection of molecules at the concentration of 1 in 10^{-8} molar. This makes possible the detection of the equivalent of a cube of sugar in a lake several square miles in area. It also has a great potential for monitoring the environment and detecting ecological changes.

46

Biotechnology's elucidation of oncogenes has provided important insights into the process involved in the development of cancer and the potential for new quantitative diagnostics. In animal health care, agents for the prophylaxis of a number of serious diseases are already being sold. For example, interferon could affect shipping fever, a disease which takes a heavy toll when cattle are moved around. Milk production is now safely improved by products not yet on the market, through the use of bovine growth hormone.

Finally, there are vaccines in development for major viral diseases. Some of these would offer safety advantages over classic vaccines because live viruses would not be introduced into the food chain; rather, protection is provided by developing antibodies to viral peptides.

There has been progress in introducing new genes into plants and controlling their expression. For example, soybean plants have been innoculated with a genetically altered rhizobium, resulting in greatly increased efficiency of nitrogen fixation. The plant's need for fertilizer is reduced, with an ecological benefit that could expand food production.

Finally, magic bullets, which carry toxins and other chemical agents directly to specific sites of disease, are already in human clinical trials. An example is the genetic engineering of erythropoietin. Erythropoietin was first defined in 1905, yet it took advanced biotechnology to produce it. Erythropoietin causes the production of red blood cells in a mouse to increase 50 percent in about two weeks. By analogy, in man, one milligram of human erythropoietin would be the equivalent of providing a patient with two units of blood for transfusion. It would be perfectly matched blood, without the introduction of any foreign proteins or the risk of infection. This very exciting opportunity is made possible entirely through genetic engineering.

Facing the practical problems

Are there practical problems in implementing biotechnology? Can sufficient quantities of these materials be made? With gamma interferon, 225,000 doses of the drug can be made in one production run by using a 300-liter fermenter. That suggests a production feasibility that perhaps many people have not realized is now at hand. Although the purification process is tedious, it is relatively straightforward. It is possible to produce the mentioned pharmaceuticals in the quantities necessary to meet world demand. I believe there is clear evidence on the scientific side that the promise of biotechnology has been met.

What is forecast for the 1985 to 1990 period? As before, there are different estimates. There is the high probability that biotechnology will have an impact on cardiovascular disease, renal carcinomas, anemias, hemophilias, and viral diseases.

Commercially, there is a very interesting phenomenon. Many relationships have developed between Japanese companies and non-Japanese biotechnology firms. This is recognition that the United States not only has produced and met the goals of the promise of biotechnology, but has been acknowledged as the world leader.

This U.S. lead, in my opinion, is a result of the support of biological research by the National Institutes of Health. Between 1978 and 1983, the NIH awarded a total of 4,700 grants. Prior to this period, the U.S. government laid the foundation for this science; government grants for biomedical research attracted people of quality to work in this field and enabled the manpower pool to develop effectively. This is one of the most significant contributions to the current U.S. lead.

Another contribution is the National Institutes of Health Recombinant DNA Advisory Committee (RAC). The RAC developed and administered the guidelines of the National Institutes of Health for conducting research with recombinant DNA in an enlightened and conscientious way. Other contributions are the venture capital system, which generated billions of dollars, and a strong, effective partnership between academic, industrial, and government scientists and administration. In addition, society has been the beneficiary of a highly motivated, brilliant group of scientists who at present are mostly in the United States.

U.S. leadership

Biotechnology research is continuing, with or without a leadership position by the United States. What are the critical factors necessary to maintain this leadership and to move ahead? Although I do not think there is any way to quantify it, it would appear that the Japanese commitment far exceeds anything going on in the United States. Yet the U.S. commitment is certainly a very big commitment. For example, in 1983, Paine-Webber estimates R&D expenditures in the United States of the biotechnology industry as a whole, of about $236 million. They further estimate a market capitalization of about $1.6 billion. In fact the total expenditure in this country for biotechnology in just the pharmaceutical industry accounts for 10 percent of R&D.

Fulfilling biotechnology's promise

What is needed to maintain momentum in a field? One needs financing, talent, and opportunity. It appears that the talent, the opportunity, and the finances are present in the United States. How can the odds of maintaining U.S. leadership be increased? Several options are evident. Support research and support development. It is not clear whether development should be government supported or left up to private capital, as it has been in the past. Develop R&D tax incentives. Tax breaks should be sustained or appropriately expanded. These options are targeted to support and stimulate the biotechnology industry.

Other courses of action would reduce the barriers that the biotechnology industry perceives to exist and that introduce additional time and cost into the process of doing business. For example, evaluate the patent process. When patent issues remain in doubt, it is hard to make the commitments to move products into the marketplace. Export barriers should be reduced. There are products that apply overseas very effectively, but at the present time there are major barriers to exporting such products. As a result, biotechnology firms are induced to work with overseas partners so that they can manufacture the materials and are not forced to export from this country. Finally, there should be an expeditious regulatory process. There is always the implication and possibility that industry wants to shortcut safety considerations. But nobody wants to shortcut safety considerations; it is a very poor strategy for the long term.

Other options are not typical of the way the United States has operated in the past, for example, the use of national targets. Most members of the Industrial Biotechnology Association would not feel it was useful to have a national goal. On this point, I think there is uniform agreement.

The United States could maintain leadership in biotechnology, but, should it? To answer that question one asks, what are the best alternatives to biotechnology for confronting the world's problems in disease, nutrition, congenital defects, environment, aging, energy, and others? Most people have not come up with very good alternatives to biotechnology. Biotechnology could still slow down in the hopes that other alternatives present themselves. However, I think society would have to address how to deal with those individuals whose only hope today is the potential impact of biotechnology on their specific problems.

The United States can develop a process to move ahead safely and rapidly, simply by maintaining the momentum of the past and not introducing new constraints that could have a negative impact. Such a process would have the full support of all the participants in the biotechnology industry. It would be a great step toward proving the reality of the futuristic promises of biotechnology.

Comments by Jack Doyle

THERE ARE some very significant choices to make regarding the potential of biotechnology in agriculture. First, there is a major opportunity to reduce the use of chemical pesticides in the environment. There have been promises of genes being engineered into crops to make them insect and disease resistant. There have also been promises of manmade "good bugs" fighting bad bugs such as Monsanto's new microbial pesticide. If these products can be brought to market safely, they will help reduce the load of toxic chemicals in the environment. And today, especially in the shadow of the recent disaster in Bhopal, such promises need to be considered with a new fervor. Bhopal exemplifies the extensive nature of the chemical system, from factory production on the one hand and worker exposures, to the application of the products in the field and broader public exposures on the other.

Although there is a dramatic opportunity to apply some of the new genetic technologies in a constructive way to reduce pesticide toxicity in the environment, I urge extreme caution with biotechnology in the microbial realm. It is very, very important for the Environmental Protection Agency and other agencies to have a predictive ecology in place before genetically engineered microbial products are released into the environment. It is also very important that a neutral, public-sector science capability be in hand as the new era of commercial biotechnology is entered.

The public sector must play a leadership role in evaluating and pointing the way toward constructive products in biotechnology. There has already been a massive movement of scientific talent from the public sector to the commercial sphere in the field of molecular biology. Traditionally, society has relied on the university to produce a neutral base of evaluation for new products, and that neutrality is no less important now.

With those two caveats in mind—the need to proceed with caution in the microbial realm and the importance of public sector science—let us explore how biotechnology can help reduce and eliminate the pesticide system that we have lived with now for forty years. As already mentioned, one possibility is to develop crops that have been genetically engineered for disease and insect resistance. Society can look forward to the use of such crops because they will reduce the need for pesticides and will help lower the farmer's cost of production.

Another area of promise is viral insecticides. These viruses are biodegradable. They can be used in small quantities, have a long shelf life, and can be used with existing pesticide equipment. Yet to date there has been little commercial activity in viral insecticides, primarily because they serve a very tiny market. In addition, before the Supreme Court Chakrabarty decision in 1980, there was no patent protection on viruses, then regarded as a product of nature.

Another promising area where biotechnology may help is the development of alleleopathic chemicals. These chemicals, which have herbicidal effects, are produced naturally by some plants. Certain cover crops, which produce these natural herbicides, may be used in conjunction with cash crops to reduce the need for synthetic herbicides.

These are only a few of the products that might be advanced by biotechnology. What is actually being done commercially in these areas? Monsanto recently advanced a new microbial product, a genetically engineered soil bacteria that emits a toxin to kill black cutworms, which are presently a pest of corn in the Midwest. Monsanto's scientist, Bob Kaufman, mentioned at the announcement of their proposed microbial pesticide for fighting black cutworms, that with such products, it is possible that insecticides could be phased out in twenty-five years.

That comment is interesting for a couple of reasons. First, he said insecticides *could* be phased out; that does not mean they will be. Second, some might suggest that twenty-five years is too long. With this technology at hand, it might be possible to do it sooner than twenty-five years. Another important point: although the use of insecticides is now declining, the use of herbicides in the environment is rapidly increasing.

While the opportunity to reduce the chemical load on the environment with biotechnology exists, I am not optimistic that with its application the pesticide era will rapidly close. For example, at least seventeen companies are now using biotechnology in herbicide resistance work. The point of this research is to give herbicide-sensitive crops the genetic capability of resisting herbicides that are sometimes lethal to them and damaging to crop yields. I am very concerned with this application of biotechnology because it may increase the load of herbicides in the environment as well as expand the range of their use.

Some people suggest that herbicides are safer than table salt, and indeed maybe some of them are. But the fact is, not much is known about herbicide toxicity. Complete "environmental fate" data are available for only a handful of the herbicides now in use. Generally, not much is known about pesticides. Sixty to 70 percent have not been tested for their ability to cause birth defects; 90 percent have not been tested for their potential to cause genetic mutations.

Recent revelations about herbicides such as atrazine, paraquat, and alachlor in groundwater should give one pause for the kind of genetic research that we now see with making crops herbicide resistant. I think the Environmental Protection Agency should look at some of the herbicides that are now being pursued for herbicide resistance. They should take a close look at the potential toxicity of these herbicides before society is faced with products that may have to be recalled under difficult circumstances.

On a related front, a major seed company has recently asked a major chemical company for samples of its new herbicide, chlor-sulfuron. Seed company scientists are screening their new hybrid corn lines with that chemical to see if the corn lines will be resistant to the herbicide. I hope that this screening of genetic material to fit a chemical product does not become a customary practice. If such practices become the rule in the crop genetics industry, a whole new set of questions will have to be addressed, including how biotechnology may be facilitating a process that is selecting out certain other genetic traits as well. For example, might genetic traits be screened out that may be valuable for disease resistance, or for other purposes, when corn lines are screened for herbicide resistance?

In sum, although some of the research investments now occurring in biotechnology hold great promise for the environment, the work we now see going on in herbicide resistance suggests that the pesticide era in agriculture is far from over and will likely be present for at least another generation of patented products.

On that point, however, I hope to be proven wrong. I hope that the pesticide era will end sooner with the constructive and safe application of biotechnology rather than later. Yet one of the biggest obstacles to that happening is a vested interest in using the existing pesticide capital and factories to produce more pesticide products. That is why it will take twenty-five years to phase out insecticides. But there will be a change in chemistry here. Lower toxicity? Maybe. There will certainly be a more sophisticated agricultural chemistry.

The elimination of chemical toxicity in agriculture? I am not sure. This conference has focused on the questions of regulation. Yet the kind of progressive product development we are hoping to see in the future is something that cannot be regulated into existence. There may be only one "window of opportunity" to pursue some of the benign agricultural products now made possible with biotechnology. But if substantial capital investments are made in one direction, that window may be missed. I hope not.

Comments by Zsolt Harsanyi

I WOULD like to clarify what the responsible promise of biotechnology was originally. The promise was that biotechnology was going to allow us to make things in a new way—a new method of production. This can be underscored with a quote from the Office of Technology Assessment report, "The Impacts of Applied Genetics." During the study, many asked about the economic potential of the technology. The report stated, "The difficulty in predicting the economic impact is exemplified by interferon. If it is found to be broadly effective against both viral diseases and cancers, sales would be in the tens of billions of dollars annually. . . . If these potential effects were not found to hold true, the impacts would be significantly less."

The conclusion by the Office of Technology Assessment was that biotechnology offered great potential. How much of this potential can actually come to pass? Wall Street has been rather impatient. Stock prices have fallen to 50 percent of their peak level for biotechnology. Some are actually traded well below their initial public offering prices. The problem is that many people expected instant solutions, but solutions are not instantaneous.

Concerning the actual successes of biotechnology, well over 400 genes have been cloned. About 10 percent of these are human genes. Today, approximately two dozen products are in the preclinical or clinical stage of testing. Monoclonal antibodies are being tested clinically in such areas as bone marrow transplantation and in drug delivery in cancer therapy. In the area of diagnostics of infectious disease, we can now rapidly identify previously unidentifiable diseases.

The key question about government regulatory apparatus concerns what would constitute undue delay. In the early stages of all recombinant DNA and biotechnology developments, the tendency has been that because it is a new technology, it deserves undue scrutiny or exceptional scrutiny. It is my bias that this is indeed undue.

Today many are coming to the conclusion that yes, indeed, the scrutiny has been overdone, and perhaps regulation can be relaxed. Biotechnology is not a single technology, but a variety of technologies under the same rubric. These various processes have various kinds of impacts, whether environmental, health, economic, or otherwise, and each one really should be looked at very carefully. Some could be just placed in the category of being really no different from the technologies that were looked at in the past.

What should some of the guidelines for regulation be? The most important distinction would be the distinction of whether a released product is a living organism or not. To look at everything that is a product of fermentation, that is a product of an enzyme reaction of a biological process, as coming under the heading of biotechnology is to go too far. It is important to recognize what the unique characteristics are that cause us to look at something carefully. I believe that the only characteristic that is strong enough to merit special consideration is whether the organism is living or not.

Comments by Lee Miller

IN DECEMBER 1984, twelve leading biotechnology companies in the European Economic Community (EEC) met to petition the EEC on ways in which they could improve their competitiveness in biotechnology. Three things were requested.

First, the community was requested to modify its approach to regulation so that there would be a single regulatory authority for the entire European Economic Community. Second, the companies asked that the EEC improve the property rights situation. This would ensure that companies that develop new biotechnology expertise would have an opportunity to profit and to sustain the R&D needed for success. Third, companies asked that the EEC provide raw materials at world competitive prices. This would provide access to raw materials beyond the tariff barriers that have built up over the years.

These three requests are also necessary for U.S. industry to ask of the U.S. government. Yet there are additional considerations. The first one is the U.S. government support of R&D. In the very beginning, government provided a fertile seed bed for the offensive thrust that we have seen. The second is the proposal that regulation of biotechnology be managed by the existing regulatory agencies. We in Monsanto believe that the Environmental Protection Agency, the Food and Drug Administration, and the other appropriate regulatory agencies are well equipped to provide the first-class management of regulatory affairs that is needed. Third, the United States has the free enterprise system, which is going to be very hard to replicate in the EEC.

How can the overall U.S. biotechnology development be accelerated? The current ban on export of animal and human health drugs that are not approved for sale in the United States will have an increasingly negative impact on this industry. Although this ban sounds relatively innocuous, it forces the company to place the initial plant outside the United States. A company simply cannot build a major capital factory in the United States while recognizing that it cannot export or sell in the United States until that regulatory clearance is achieved. This necessity puts a company at risk of being held hostage on a no-production basis in this country. Therefore the company's decision is to build the plant outside of the United States, thereby transferring that portion of the U.S. leadership to foreign shores. I hope this is something Congress can address. I know it is something that the biotechnology industry can respond to in a very positive, responsible fashion.

Another critical area that cannot be overemphasized is the need for property rights. These are needed in order to sustain and justify the kind of research that industry is involved in.

Environmental Risks and Genetically Engineered Organisms

SIMON A. LEVIN and MARK A. HARWELL

BIOTECHNOLOGY offers tremendous potential for improving the human condition. Advances seem likely in pharmaceutical development, food processing, agricultural production, and environmental management. To achieve many of these goals will require the deliberate release into the environment of organisms whose genomes have been manipulated. The possibility of undesirable side effects to human health and to the environment will accompany such releases and, even if the great majority of introductions proves to be benign or beneficial, a single catastrophe could cast a shadow over the entire industry. By developing a reliable system to protect against mishaps, technological developments will be facilitated. Without a widely accepted and respected regulatory system, any deliberate release faces the possibility of injunctions and lawsuits.

When a society is confronted with a brand new problem, that society naturally searches its experience for similar problems to examine how and how well they were solved. In the case of deliberate releases of the products of biotechnology, there are six usual touchstones: laboratory experimentation with recombinant DNA (rDNA) and other genetic technologies; agricultural practices, including selective plant and animal breeding and biological control of pests; deliberate or accidental introductions of exotic species; epidemics and epizootics; regulation of chemical substances introduced into the environment; and ecological and evolutionary theory.

What is new? What is familiar?

Depending on one's professional training and inclinations, any of these may seem the natural starting point for approaching the problem of deliberate release. In formulating a strategy for managing deliberate releases, the relevant features must be extracted from each approach.

Funding for this research was provided by the Office of Research and Development, U.S. Environmental Protection Agency, under Cooperative Agreement CR 811060, and by Cornell University.

56

Laboratory experimentation

Laboratory experimentation with rDNA is relevant to the problem of the deliberate release of an rDNA organism because both employ a common technology. However, unlike releases to the environment, there is an effective system for guarding against accidents in the lab. Evaluation of risks associated with laboratory experimentation begins with the problem of containment and possible escape. Only secondarily must one deal with the probabilities that escaping organisms will survive in the natural environment; that they will reproduce and proliferate; and finally, that they will cause adverse health or environmental effects. Safeguards on laboratory experimentation generally are adequate to ensure that the probability of escape is very low and that potentially dangerous organisms, even if they escape, will not survive in the natural environment.

In the case of deliberate release, however, "escape" into the environment is a certainty; and survival, at least for some period of time, is essential for the introduction to be useful. Thus the first two steps in the protocol for lab experimentation are effectively bypassed. Therefore attention must be directed to those areas where there is the least information and experience: the proliferation of the deliberately released material, and the possible effects upon biota. In fact, the desire to minimize risks may be directly opposed to the intent of the introduction. For example, the ability of a released organism to grow and spread may be a deliberate objective, as release of a small quantity of material may spread its effects over a wide area, producing both an economic benefit and an obvious environmental risk. Further, many genetic alterations are aimed at modifying interspecies interactions (for example, by modifying resistance to pathogens or predators, or changing competitive ability) or system-level processes (for example, nitrogen cycling). The regulatory issues for deliberate releases clearly are fundamentally different than for controlled laboratory situations, and the probabilities of ecological side effects are much greater.

Agricultural practices

Plant and animal breeding generally has been directed toward genetic characteristics that have little influence upon the potential of the species to proliferate in the natural environment. In the unlikely case of escape of individuals from controlled environments, the likelihood of adverse effects from these technologies is minimal.[1] However, past practice does illustrate some potential

1. Philip J. Regal, "Potential Ecological Impact of Genetically Engineered Organisms," in Harold Mooney, ed., *Ecological Consequences of Biological Invasions* (New York: Springer-Verlag, forthcoming).

problems. Selection for plant varieties resistant to pests can lead to a reduction in plant diversity, and to the development of new forms of virulence in pest species. These can spread widely and rapidly.

Although regulation by the Department of Agriculture and individual states where agriculture is prominent to the economy guard against potentially catastrophic introductions, accidents occur and can have profound economic consequences, (for example, citrus canker, Mediterranean fruit fly). In recognition of these experiences, the Division of Agriculture Committee on Biotechnology of the National Association of State Universities and Land Grant Colleges has recently proposed a national biological impact assessment program for biotechnology concerning release and introduction of plant material, parasites, and predators.[2]

Prior introductions of exotics

Another agricultural practice is the intentional introduction of natural biological enemies of pest species. It is natural to seek analogies for regulating products of biotechnology with the historic events of deliberate or accidental introductions of exotic species into ecosystems or "introductions of exotics." Several recent reviews conclude that the great majority of such introductions are not successful, and many of those that are do not cause dislocations in other parts of the ecosystem.[3] However, there are many examples of introductions that have gone awry—starlings, gypsy moths, kudzu, chestnut blight, citrus canker, and others—which are cause for considerable concern.

These experiences help identify the kinds of problems that might arise with deliberate releases, yet it is difficult to extrapolate from studies on vertebrates and insects to derive conclusions about microorganisms and plants. Widely different taxa have very different characteristics of growth, reproduction, and dispersal, and play fundamentally different roles in the ecosystem. Thus we must recognize the limitations of our current data base and take

2. Division of Agriculture, Committee on Biotechnology, *Emerging Biotechnologies in Agriculture: Issues and Policies*, Progress Report 111 (Washington, D.C.: National Association of State Universities and Land Grant Colleges, 1984).

3. Robert T. Paine and Thomas M. Zaret, "Ecological Gambling: The High Risks and Rewards of Species Introduction," *Journal of the American Medical Association*, vol. 231 (1975), pp. 471–73; Daniel Simberloff, "Community Effects of Introduced Species," in Matthew H. Nitecki, ed., *Biotic Crises in Ecological and Evolutionary Time* (Academic Press, 1981), pp. 53–81; and Francis E. Sharples, *Spread of Organisms with Novel Genotypes: Thoughts from an Ecological Perspective*, Publication 2040, ORNL/TM-8473 (Oak Ridge, Tenn.: National Laboratory, Environmental Sciences Division, 1982); *Environmental Implications of Genetic Engineering*, prepared for the House Committee on Science and Technology (Government Printing Office, 1983), pp. 157–206; and *Recombinant DNA Technical Bulletin*, vol. 6 (June 1983), pp. 43–56.

steps to enlarge it to include more examples of the effects of introductions of microorganisms and plants.

There are four classes of introductions: slightly modified forms of resident types; forms that exist naturally in the target environment but that require continual supplemental support or continual replacement to be sustained; forms that exist naturally elsewhere in the environment but that previously have not reached the target environment; and genuine novelties.[4]

In the third category experience with exotics is most relevant. Even in this case, although one can talk about probabilities of establishment, it is difficult to draw generalizations beyond the crude observation that opportunistic species are most likely to succeed, and that simple and disturbed or polluted habitats are most vulnerable.[5]

Epidemics and epizootics

Examining the history of epidemics and epizootics provides a line of evidence whose relevance has not been recognized fully. For example, the versatile influenza virus illustrates the potential for genetic change and consequent major catastrophe. New strains of influenza virus arise frequently. The Influenza-A strains differ by only a few surface antigens produced by genetic mutation or recombination. Yet these changes are sufficient to produce new immunologically distinct strains. If there is insufficient immunity in the population, these new strains have the potential to spread through the population, causing untold suffering. Thus a very small genetic alteration can make a major ecological difference.

Similarly, the potential for rapid growth, proliferation, and evolutionary changes in populations of microorganisms is very well illustrated by the history of myxomatosis in Australia. The European rabbit, introduced into Australia, became a major pest species until the myxoma virus was introduced as a control measure.[6] Within a year or two, the virus (which causes a fatal infection in rabbits) had done its work, and the rabbit was nearly eliminated. This story has been seen as one of the great successes of biological control. However, within a few years after the initial

4. Simon A. Levin and Mark A. Harwell, "Potential Ecological Consequences of Genetically Engineered Organisms," in J.W. Gillett and others, *Potential Impacts of Environmental Release of Biotechnology Products: Assessment, Regulation, and Research Needs*, ERC-075 (Cornell University, Ecosystems Research Center, 1985), pp. 104–36.

5. Sharples, *Spread of Organisms with Novel Genotypes*; "Environmental Implications of Genetic Engineering," prepared for the House Committee on Science and Technology; and *Recombinant DNA Technical Bulletin*, pp. 43–56.

6. Frank Fenner, "Biological Control As Exemplified by Smallpox Eradication and Myxomatosis," 1983 Florey Lecture, *Proceedings of the Royal Society of London*, series B, vol. 218, pp. 259–85.

success, the myxoma virus had evolved to a much less virulent form, and the rabbit population had begun to recover. This evolution, and the subsequent evolution of resistance in the rabbit population, has caused some to worry that the time is approaching when the myxoma virus will cease to be an effective tool for control.

The influenza and myxoma examples demonstrate the potential for microorganisms to spread rapidly and cause major effects on ecosystems, as well as the tremendous genetic volatility of populations of microorganisms. The popular view, that what we see in natural communities is the end product of hundreds of millions of years of evolution and highly resistant to change, is fallacious.[7] Natural communities are dynamic evolutionary assemblages with great potential to respond to new stresses.

The regulation of chemicals

The introduction of chemicals into ecosystems raises similar regulatory problems to those of biotechnology. As for biotic introductions, one needs a testing system to assess the fate of the introduced chemical material—how it will be changed and where it will be moved—and the potential effects on ecosystems.

There are major differences between the considerations for chemicals and those for biological introductions. The latter have a great capacity for geographical spread far beyond the point of application, and for proliferation by reproduction. Moreover, the genetic information is often carried on plasmids (movable pieces of DNA that can be exchanged between individuals and even between species). This adds new dimensions to the problems of exposure assessment and the fate of the new genetic material. Many proposed biotechnology introductions are targeted to affect directly fundamental system processes, such as nitrification, nitrogen fixation, or decomposition. The possibility of ecological effects upon these functions therefore becomes a matter of direct effects rather than indirect ones, contrasted with the usual situation involving chemicals.

Ecological theory

Ecological theory provides no general answers to the problems at hand, and it is dangerous to expect simple remedies. The oft-stated principle that ecological systems are resilient and can withstand any perturbation clearly is not supported by fact. Rather, there is much anecdotal information to the contrary. For specific systems, it is to be expected that the insights of an experienced

7. Regal, "Potential Ecological Impact of Genetically Engineered Organisms."

ecologist would provide more valuable counsel concerning potential effects than reliance on general rules.

Natural systems are evolutionarily dynamic. Strong selective forces, such as those provided by highly toxic substances, for example, heavy metals and pesticides, exploit the genetic variability of natural populations. For example, the rapid evolution of heavy metal tolerance by organisms near deposits of mine tailings and of pesticide resistance among pest species has been documented. Similarly, bacteria may evolve antibiotic resistance. Another example is provided by fungal pathogens that rapidly overcome the fungal resistance bred into agricultural crops such as cereals. Microorganisms have an especially high potential for change because of their rapid population turnover rates.

In general, the evolutionary process may be seen as a combination of forces that generate variability (for example, mutation and recombination) and those that operate on that variability to select the favored types (for example, by natural selection). The rate of evolution is dependent upon the amount of variability for a particular trait within a population and upon the strength of the selective force. The fact that most mutations are deleterious to the individual does not deter the evolutionary process; natural selection simply chooses the few that are beneficial. Similar arguments apply to introductions of genetically engineered species. The fact that many will fail is less important than the fact that those few that succeed might spread rapidly and displace indigenous types.

It is often stated that the introduction of genetically engineered species is similar to the process of mutation that generates variability. But there are important quantitative differences. Biotechnology increases the mutation rate and can provide strong artificial selection regimes. These may effect rapid evolutionary change and the destabilization of coevolved complexes of species.

In summary, five factors unique to deliberate release of genetically modified organisms can be identified:

—The modification of the ecological role of a microorganism is often the direct objective of biotechnology. The wide geographical range and high dispersal capability of many of the proposed targets of biotechnology suggest that introductions may proliferate widely if they escape beyond the initial area of release.

—The problems of escape from containment and of survival are not at issue when release is deliberate, and survival is enhanced by genetic engineering. Regulation should focus on the potential for proliferation and upon ecological effects.

—Introduction of genuinely novel organisms into the environment is not analogous to the introductions of exotics that are simply transferred from other environments. However, even when such exotics are well known and introduced into well-studied systems, uncertainties remain and long-term predictions may not be reliable.

—Biological introductions into the environment differ from the introduction of toxic substances because of the capacity of life forms to grow and multiply.

—Concern should be directed to the spread of deliberately released organisms, and to the spread of their genetic information, both vertically (by inheritance) and horizontally (by infectious transfer).

The cumulative effects of a suite of deliberate releases also must be considered. For example, in the case of toxic chemicals, the sequential introduction of new materials provides a situation in which any single introduction may be considered to be acceptable in risk, but also in which the cumulative effects of multiple low-level stresses are unacceptable. Current regulatory approaches do not provide an adequate mechanism for dealing with such cumulative effects.

Fate, transport, and ecological effects

Ecological issues that are relevant to the problem of deliberate release include fate, transport, and ecological effects.[8]

Fate and Transport

Any assessment of the effects of an introduction must involve the fate and transport of the introduced material—where it goes, how it is transformed, and what populations are exposed to its effects. For biological introductions, attention must be directed to growth, dispersal, and plasmid transfer events.

Martin Alexander reviews what is known about the survival and growth of bacteria in the environment, detailing the extrinsic factors (seasonality, temperature, pH, and so on), and biological characteristics (tolerance levels, competitive ability) that govern the success of bacterial populations in natural settings.[9] The present data base is sparse, and it is critical to enlarge upon it. Similarly, David A. Andow reviews the literature concerning the dispersal

8. Simon A. Levin and Mark A. Harwell, "Potential Ecological Consequences of Genetically Engineered Organisms"; Gillett and others, *Potential Impacts of Environmental Release of Biotechnology Products*; and Simon A. Levin and Kenneth D. Kimball, eds., and W.H. McDowell and S.F. Kimball, assoc. eds., "New Perspectives in Ecotoxicology," *Environmental Management*, vol. 8, no. 5 (1984), pp. 375–442.

9. Martin Alexander, "Survival and Growth of Bacteria," in Gillett and others, *Potential Impacts of Environmental Release of Biotechnology Products*, pp. 49–62.

of microorganisms, with special attention to the various modes of transmission.[10] Here the factors of major influence are the initial source pool size, the effectiveness of the dispersal agent, and the susceptibility of the target environment.

Although such studies provide a starting point for consideration of the effects of particular introductions, a testing and screening procedure that allows case-by-case consideration of any introduction is essential. Microcosms provide a promising technology for evaluating both growth and plasmid transfer, since microorganisms can be studied under controlled and safe conditions, in systems that are of manageable size. For dispersal, extrapolation from the literature and mathematical models will be necessary.

Ecological Effects

Attention must be paid to possible effects upon other species, as well as upon the structure and function of the ecosystem. In general, it is not possible to make long-term predictions about effects of a particular stress upon the dynamics of particular populations, much less on community structure or on ecosystem functions. Thus any attempt at prediction must be viewed as a crude approximation, and reliability decreases rapidly as the time period under consideration increases. This underscores the desirability of coupling monitoring with management, so that management can be "adapted" as information accrues.[11] In the case of deliberate releases, errors must be expected, and the means for their mitigation must be available.

Special attention must be directed to those cases in which the application of biotechnology is intended to affect directly ecological processes such as primary and secondary production and nutrient cycling. This is especially important because many of the targeted species play essential roles in ecosystem processes and have broad geographical ranges.

Conclusions for regulation

A sound regulatory system for the deliberate release of the products of biotechnology must include the following:

—An assessment before the deliberate release of a new organism of the fate and transport of genetic information, and of possible

10. David A. Andow, "Dispersal of Microorganisms with Novel Genotypes," in Gillett and others, *Potential Impacts of Environmental Release of Biotechnology Products*, pp. 63–103.

11. Crawford Holling, *Adaptive Environmental Assessment and Management* (Wiley, 1978); and Karin E. Limburg, Christine C. Harwell, and Simon A. Levin, *Principles for Estuarine Impact Assessment: Lessons Learned from the Hudson River and Other Estuarine Experiences*, ERC–024 (Cornell University, Ecosystems Research Center, 1984).

effects on the biota and on system processes in the affected environment;

—Monitoring after the release of the introduced organism of its fate, transport, and effects;

—A plan for containment of the introduced organism within predefined geographical limits; and

—Contingency plans for mitigation in case of undesirable side effects.

These four needs are not independent of each other and an integrated plan should involve each. There are a variety of possible schemes for developing an integrated plan. The simplest approach involves a preliminary assessment of possible short-term effects in the absence of mitigation, and of the potential for mitigation, followed by successive refinement of the various components, utilizing information gained from the other pieces.

One goal should be a ranking of risks associated with various introductions on the basis of the nature of the genetic manipulation (for example, does the engineering involve movable elements?); the immediate health or ecological effects (survival in and effects upon mammalian species; pathogenicity; effects on nutrient cycling, lignin degradation); and factors related to the potential for limitation of effects and possible mitigation (temporal and spatial scales, host range, habitat specificity, dispersal capabilities, antibiotic resistance, dependence on external subsidies, availability of controls). No single technology suffices for this purpose, and the development of an integrated program of laboratory and microcosm testing, mathematical modeling, extrapolation from data bases, and limited and carefully controlled field testing must represent a top research priority.

A safe regulatory process that will not inhibit technological and economic development will involve a tiered screening system. During the early tiers, relatively simple tests aimed at weeding out the most obvious risks can be accomplished. Later tiers would involve more expensive and more complicated ecological tests dictated by the findings from the earlier tests.[12] It is well within our reach to develop such a system. We cannot afford not to do so.

Comments by Frank E. Young

IN THE Midsummer Night's Dream, the character Snout says, "In this strange interlude, it doth befall that I, one Snout by name,

12. Levin and Kimball, eds., and McDowell and Kimball, assoc. eds., "New Perspectives in Ecotoxicology"; and Kenneth D. Kimball and Simon A. Levin, "Limitations of Laboratory Bioassays: The Need for Ecosystem-level Testing," *Bioscience*, vol. 35, no. 3 (1985), pp. 165–71.

portray a wall." In dealing with this strange interlude of regulating biotechnology, I might say "It doth befall that I, one Young by name, portray the fallibility of the faith in regulations."

In this strange interlude of regulation, the ability to look at and possibly deem correct the type of regulation is unclear. Thus a very cautious case-by-case method of dealing with the analysis of risks at the time of deliberate release of microorganisms into the environment is needed.

The following issues must be considered. It is imperative to distinguish between real and imagined risks. It is not fair to the American people to make up a long list of possibilities and put them on the wall without giving some degree of probability therein. A cardinal rule in microbial genetics is the variability of species and the capacity of organisms to deal with and change in their host-parasite relationships. Thus understanding the predator-prey issues is extraordinarily important.

The range of exchange of genetic material between microorganisms is another concern. It is important not only to consider the range of genetic exchange in plasmids, but also the range of genetic exchange among viruses. It is important to recognize that in most systems the range of exchange of genetic information is very narrow and is restricted by biological mechanisms (for example, transformation, transduction, and conjugation).

Another concern in a case-by-case analysis is the careful examination of the ecological niche in which the organism resides. During the past few decades a great deal has been learned about a few model organisms, for example, *Escherichia coli*, and soil organisms such as *Bacillus subtilis*. But as we move from these model systems, we have substantial ignorance. One of the greater concerns is an understanding of the amount of research that's required to build a broad platform for this particular type of deliberate release analysis.

Finally, I focus on the process of risk analysis. The Food and Drug Administration has been dealing with biotechnological developments for the past three or four years, particularly in devices and in medicinals, on a case-by-case analysis. Though the Food and Drug Administration has not had to deal with the environmental concerns, the principles used to determine risk are the same. The following need to be answered: what is the organism under consideration? How is the genetic technology done? What is the degree of stability of the genetic elements? To what extent will they survive in the environment; to what extent will they spread in the environment? And to what extent will regulation be able to determine an up-front risk? Answering these questions requires a case-by-case analysis that confounds the development of integrated, detailed regulations. Such regulation would take away some of the broader scope of human judgments that I believe are critical. Regulators must proceed certainly in the face of uncertainty. I submit this can be done on a case-by-case basis.

Comments by David A. Jackson

THE PRESENT debate on the risks of genetically engineered organisms has focused on the deliberate release of these organisms into the natural environment, and the appropriate regulatory environment in which these releases might occur. In my judgment, this debate is in danger of being misled. Many have assumed that such organisms, whether a microbe, a plant, or an animal, represent something fundamentally new and different because of genetic engineering. This assumption is incorrect. Genetic engineering is part of a continuum of genetic modifications that man has been making to organisms for a long time, for example, the domestication of plants and animals. Genetic engineering techniques can be viewed simply as a more efficient means of modification than have been accomplished by the more expensive, time-consuming, and less efficient conventional processes of mutation, selection, and breeding programs.

There are many different technologies within biotechnology, only one of which is genetic engineering. Regulatory action regarding the products produced by biotechnology should be directed toward the properties of the products and not toward the technology used for production. The existing underlying regulatory agencies and statutory authorities are an appropriate base from which to regulate products made by using biotechnology, including genetic engineering.

A ban on all controlled introductions of genetically engineered organisms into the environment would be counterproductive, both scientifically and as public policy. It is in the interest of the country to commercialize biotechnology in a responsible way and to preserve our lead relative to other countries in this extremely important technology.

In the mid-1970s, in response to a controversy about the potential biohazards of genetically engineered microorganisms, the Asilomar Conference was held. As a result, those involved in Asilomar learned that scientific input from many disciplines is extremely important in considering questions of potential risks.

It was also learned that open public discussions of the risks and the benefits and the evidence that are relevant to these questions are essential for the process to be accepted within a political context. Molecular geneticists do not have all or even most of the answers that are required to inform responsible regulatory policy in all of the areas on which genetic engineering has an impact. In the present case of controlled release of genetically engineered organisms into the environment, it is clear that several scientific disciplines, besides molecular genetics and ecology, need to be involved. The Asilomar experience showed that it was not until specialists in infectious disease, epidemiology, and public health were brought into discussion with molecular geneticists and biochemists that it was possible to quiet much of the uninformed noise that had hindered real progress and to resolve controversial questions. Resolution of these issues was quite contentious. But it was possible because people had the facts to say what was real about many issues of potential biohazard.

It is relatively easy to set up scientific paradigms—experiments that can test the underlying assumptions for some of the more horrible scenarios that were being put forth. The experiments that formed many of the assumptions that underlay the horrible scenarios were simply not valid. These results reassured many people, including a lot of people in molecular biology communities, whose intuition had told them that the potential problems were being greatly exaggerated. Fortunately, it is often rather simple to identify and perform a few key experiments, the data from which one can clarify major questions and provide the basis of intelligent future action.

Society cannot insist on zero risk. Society has to be willing to accept some risk in order to gain information that will provide the basis for greater certainty about risk and safety. The only way of getting such data is by performing experiments. By definition, one does not know how an experiment is going to come out ahead of time. The scientific community should be getting on with the job of identifying and performing the key experiments relating to large-scale release of genetically modified organisms, so that regulatory policy having a sound, factual base will be possible.

The issue of potential risks to the environment caused by the introductions of new organisms or chemicals is obviously one that must be taken seriously. There will surely be some situations in which such introductions will be harmful. The real issue is what fraction of the organisms will present potential problems;

how great those problems will be; how easy it will be to predict and then either avoid or control them; and what the potential benefits and their associated probability may be.

Even the severest critics of the introduction of genetically engineered organisms into the environment concede that there will be little or no problem in the vast majority of cases. Since no one is doing these introductions just for fun, I think one has to conclude that the vast majority of such introductions are expected to be beneficial and will present relatively little risk. How can those relatively rare cases where there may be serious problems, and where increased care and scrutiny are warranted before any release is attempted be identified?

The scientific community could try to identify generic problems that are likely to occur in the release of relatively novel organisms and get research started. If generic problems can be identified, that will be a great advantage, because it means that not every organism needs to be analyzed on a case-by-case basis, as I think is necessary at the beginning. Past experience in science predicts that one can expect to be able to define classes of problems in designing these experiments and to gather data on those classes so that one will be able to make decisions more efficiently.

Comments by Anne K. Vidaver

THESE REMARKS are confined to agriculture, to plants, and microorganisms associated with agriculture. The United States has the most productive and efficient agriculture in the world. This came about through deliberate experimentation with both plants and microorganisms, particularly within the last one hundred years. I contend that there is a data base in agriculture to use in analyzing the risks of deliberate release of some plants and microorganisms. This is not to say that further knowledge is not required. It is simply my opinion that some of the alarmist scenarios that are presented are not warranted.

Drawing analogies between deliberate release of genetically engineered microorganisms and introductions that have gone awry may not be appropriate because some of the introductions were not intentionally introduced, for example, chestnut blight or the citrus canker in Florida. These problematic introductions were a result of natural forces, resulting in natural epidemics. The world is evolving and is dynamic, and there will be problems in the environment, regardless of whether the subject is agriculture, human medicine, or any other activity in which biological organisms live.

The introduction of entirely novel organisms is also not an appropriate analogy. With respect to risk assessment, when talking about the release of plants or microorganisms in agriculture, the subject is really about modified organisms that will in fact be suitable for the particular environment in which they are to be used. Our whole system of agriculture is in fact based on the deliberate introduction, albeit accidentally by our ancestors, of all the crops currently grown in the United States.

Concerning the issue of safety, agriculture has been practiced experimentally for at least one hundred years. I cannot find any evidence that there has been any epidemic as a result of such experimentation. Scientists have been working under conditions in which, theoretically, epidemics could have occurred, but in fact they have not. Therefore, I contend that the testing is predictive with respect to safety and, again, can be applied to concerns about agricultural organisms.

The question of single gene resistance as a concern of rapid evolution has been raised. It is a concern but, for example, plant breeders have been able to produce cereals in higher volume and higher yields than ever before, despite this constraint. Modern biotechnology has the potential to try to understand the molecular basis for this resistance and to alleviate it.

The question of transport of introduced microorganisms has been legitimately raised. Yet some organisms in the environment do not travel very far. These organisms (both pathogens and biological control agents) can be effectively contained within a restricted environment. Many organisms have been worked with in the open for many years, providing examples of organisms that can be and are being contained in natural environments.

The question has been raised that genetic transfer can occur in the environment, particularly with plasmids. I would not dispute that. Certainly it occurs in some select situations in which there is very high population pressure. There must also be closely related organisms present in the environment. This is in contrast to laboratory situations, where one can manipulate the transfer even to unrelated organisms in many cases. The fact is that apparently in many cases, there is great stability of plasmids, as illustrated by plasmid profile analyses of naturally occurring bacteria.

With respect to plant release, I think the majority of scientists would agree that containment with plants is going to be much easier than with other kinds of organisms. Plasmids can be seen and regulated in their growth, their seed development, and harvest. With respect to cloning vectors for plants, here we have principally plant pathogens or their derivatives. We have been working on these types of organisms for at least a quarter of a century; we have a predictive capability with regard to these organisms. Most of you are familiar with crown gall. The first genetically engineered plants, in which a foreign gene was introduced into a plant, occurred with the use of a plasmid from a plant pathogen.

One must examine the facts with respect to agriculture as now practiced. Existing regulations and statutes suffice at present, and I am comfortable with the recommendations to consider deliberate releases of engineered organisms on a case-by-case basis. Initially I do not see any other way to do this, owing to the complexity of the microorganisms, plants, and the environment. But I do hope, eventually, that some general principles can be accepted.

With respect to proposed regulations, I predict that these would be highly detrimental to both basic and applied research.[1] Particularly, I am speaking of what I consider undue restrictions that are suggested for field tests. These would lead to undue delay for using technology that will ultimately be of benefit to agriculture. It is my hope that a consensus will be reached to enable reasonable experimentation to go forward.

Comments by Daniel L. Hartl

THE DIVERSITY of living organisms is unimaginable. The diversity of interactions between living organisms is also unimaginable. To a molecular biologist, it is apparent that the number of ways in which an organism can be changed is infinitely large. Thus the question, "Should we permit the introduction, into a random environment, of a random organism changed in a random way?" is not sufficiently well defined to argue sensibly. This makes me a strong advocate of the view that all introductions have to be considered on a case-by-case basis, at least at the present time.

There is sometimes an undercurrent of mutual mistrust among biologists from different subdisciplines. This mistrust reflects the different approach that molecular biologists have to the problem of environmental risks of deliberate release, than do ecologists. The attitudes can be stereotyped as follows.

To an ecologist, a molecular biologist is the ultimate simplifier, the ultimate reductionist, who not only loses the forest for the trees, but who claims there is no forest. The molecular biologist is the ultimate manipulator who thinks one knows enough to be

1. "Proposal for a Coordinated Framework for Regulation of Biotechnology," *Federal Register*, vol. 49 (December 31, 1984), pp. 50881–92.

able to change the world in a beneficial way and not take any significant risk.

To a molecular biologist, the ecologist is the ultimate dreamer, the romantic who imagines that systems that are as complex as biological communities could ever be understood to a level of developing a predictive theory. To a molecular biologist, the ecologist is the ultimate conservator who is by nature against intervention of any sort.

This argument has been going on for a very long period of time, mainly in the halls of academe, where it did not matter much. But things have changed with the prospect of the release of genetically engineered organisms into the environment. All of a sudden, the stakes have become large.

The proposal has been raised that genetically engineered organisms can be considered under the rubric of toxic substances and, as such, controlled. That analogy is extremely misleading and is likely to engender unwarranted fears on the part of the public. The vast majority of genetically engineered organisms are not toxic substances. The organisms do not produce toxins; the genetically engineered version thereof does not produce a toxin; nor could these things conceivably become toxins. Thus putting all genetically engineered organisms in the category of toxic substances for purposes of regulation, would, in my opinion, result in unnecessarily burdensome regulations.

Another point relevant to the deliberate release of genetically engineered organisms concerns the process of evolution. There are two phases of evolution; one has to do with the generation of genetic variability, largely through the processes of mutation and recombination. Genetic engineering can be considered a fancy form of humanmade mutation. The second phase of evolution concerns selection. I am impressed with how extremely difficult it seems to be for an organism to undergo favorable mutation. There are a few cases, some of which have been cited (for example, influenza virus, antibiotic resistant bacteria, pesticide resistance, or insecticide resistance in insects). Yet, in fact, the way evolution really works on a day-to-day basis is that it is very, very slow, and organisms change only over hundreds of millions of years. The probability that a random change in an organism will produce a form that is better in its environment and its competitive ability than a form that is already there—even including engineered organisms that might have been selected to perform reasonably well—is almost vanishingly small. This is a feature of the way organisms are built and the way they evolve that favors the thinking that the risks of most types of deliberate release would be negligible.

Rarely are organisms limited in their ability to grow and reproduce by individual genes, or even small groups of genes. They are usually limited by competition from other organisms and factors of climate. Thus it is very unlikely that, by inadvertence, a genetic engineer could change a gene that removes limits to the population growth of an organism.

Surely there is a need for regulation and examination of the release of genetically engineered organisms in the environment. There is a sufficient amount of knowledge to do it sensibly and rationally, and I think that at this early stage proposals should be evaluated on a case-by-case basis.

Balancing Risks and Benefits

BERNADINE HEALY BULKLEY

THE WORLD famous physicist, Freeman Dyson, entitled his autobiography *Disturbing the Universe* after a T. S. Eliot poem: "And indeed, there will be time to wonder, do I dare? Time to turn back and descend the stair, with a bald spot in the middle of my hair, do I dare? Dare disturb the universe?"

A number of points relevant to a discussion of biotechnology are made in *Disturbing the Universe* by Dyson, who witnessed the cracking of the atom and closely followed the cracking of the gene. First, science and technology move forward. They should not and cannot be restrained.

Second, science and technology are unpredictable. There is no way to reliably label them as good or bad ahead of time. If one could, one could regulate technology quite easily and with ultimate wisdom. We must continually realize that society will never have that ultimate, final knowledge that eliminates all uncertainty. Science moves forward because of unanswered questions.

Third, somewhere below the level of reason lurks a concern that new knowledge and technology can be either a destroyer or a deliverer. In many ways, this drives much of the dialogue about this so-called biological revolution: the ancient myths of good and evil, and the human desire to control how these forces disturb the universe.

This brings me to balancing risks and benefits within an institutional framework for decisionmaking. Society's concerns about technology are addressed by public scrutiny, airing public concerns, full public dialogue, and regulations by public servants within the framework of the U.S. government and its laws. A central theme is that of the public controlling the applications of science, and not science itself.

The federal government has major responsibility for the health and environmental safety consequences of technological innovation, particularly as such technologic advances emerge in the marketplace with opportunity for broad impact on society. For

73

biotechnology, the benefits to society appear particularly wide-spread, with diverse opportunities for new and better medicines and therapies for disease; better and more efficient food production; a wide range of chemicals for consumer and industrial uses; and even the promise of new sources of energy. There are also risks accompanying any of these new products. Some risks are real, some are imagined, and some are as yet unimaginable. Balancing risks and benefits case by case is a difficult but necessary task of government. Such decisionmaking requires an orderly mechanism, including agreed-on principles, statutory authority, and an institutional framework.

For biotechnology there has been little question about the responsibility and the authority of the federal government as selected cases are presented. Although DNA was first seen as the chemical basis of heredity by Oswald Avery in the 1940s, it was not until 1973 that samples of DNA from two different organisms were recombined in a directed fashion. Splicing enzymes were used to create, relatively speaking, a new life form.

This manmade transformation of living organisms in the research laboratory was almost immediately recognized as having great commercial potential and potential for wide-ranging benefit. But, scientists themselves cautioned about potential risks. The subsequent series of conferences, and the formation of the National Institutes of Health Recombinant DNA Advisory Committee (RAC) under the leadership of Dr. Donald Frederickson, who was then the director of the National Institutes of Health, are well known.

DNA advisory committee

From its inception in 1974, the RAC provided an institutional framework for balancing risks and benefits. The RAC, using a case-by-case approach, developed generic guidelines for conduct of recombinant DNA (rDNA) research that established safety standards for research activity. A mechanism for technical review was established; principles were agreed upon in terms of both the risks and the benefits; and the federal authority to do so was quite clear. Any application funded by the National Institutes of Health had to comply with the NIH review and guidelines. Since most of the basic research was supported by the NIH, the authority was adequate to meet the needs of most research.

Coincidentally, virtually all the major companies conducting basic DNA research voluntarily sought the advice of the RAC and complied with its guidelines. Thus the National Institutes of Health for a time served as a centralized framework for risk review that functioned extremely well for laboratory-based rDNA activities. It functioned so well that it even acquired the reputation of a regulatory body. Yet it never ceased to be just a scientific body whose good advice alone was so forceful that compliance with its review occurred without statutory authority.

This history is important to a discussion of how to balance risks and benefits of modern biotechnology in today's setting. Today applications of biotechnology in health care, agriculture, veterinary medicine, waste management, energy production, and for manufacture of a wide range of chemicals for household and industrial uses are emerging. These are applications requiring testing outside of the contained laboratory setting. In some cases they require new engineering processes for commercial scale up, and also new approaches to waste disposal. Assessment of efficacy and safety of these new processes and products is still necessary, but the natural question arose some time ago—who would provide the review of applied biotechnology that would allow the field to flourish, yet balance risks and safety along the way?

The National Institutes of Health Recombinant DNA Advisory Committee has been enormously successful in reviewing basic biotechnology. Could it accommodate the needs of commercial biotechnology? For commercial products—foods, drugs, and chemicals—there was clearly established statutory responsibility in several federal agencies. Questions of authority, overlapping jurisdiction, gaps in authority, adequacy of the safety review mechanism, coordination among agencies, and the continued role of the RAC superimposed on a desire by virtually all inside and outside of government to see an orderly framework for decision-making in biotechnology led to the establishment in the spring of 1984 of the White House's Cabinet Council Working Group on Biotechnology.

Cabinet council working group
The working group operated under several premises. The group believed that biotechnology is good and that the safety of new products and processes must be adequately assessed. The group also felt that the United States is currently the world leader in biotechnology largely because of the U.S. investment in basic research and that it should maintain that leadership as biotechnology products are commercialized. It became apparent that the first issues for the working group to address were the real or perceived regulatory uncertainties and inefficiencies. Would federal regulation adversely affect the climate for innovation and leadership in biotechnology? Would federal regulation generate concern in the public that its safety was not being adequately protected?

Accordingly the group's first task was to outline a coordinated interagency framework for regulation of biotechnology. That initial effort was summarized in the *Federal Register*.[1]

The report consists of three major sections. The first is a matrix that describes existing laws, regulations, and guidelines that may be applicable to biotechnology products and processes. These are shown as they apply at each point in the sequence of research, development, manufacturing, marketing, shipping, and disposal. A glance at nineteen pages of tables might suggest that there is rather ample federal authority to regulate biotechnology.

The second part of the report contains policy statements by the Environmental Protection Agency, the Food and Drug Administration, and the Department of Agriculture. These are the agencies most extensively involved in oversight of biotechnology products. They attempt to clarify the policies of these agencies. The agencies expand on the statutes that provide regulatory authority and outline the general policy framework within which regulatory decisions will be made. They attempt to provide clearer understanding of how regulatory agencies will approach this emerging and changing field.

The first common step, stated in each agency's policy statements, is to determine authority to regulate in a given area. That determination is based for the most part upon the uses or characteristics of the products. When a new kind of product is developed, each agency must apply its guidelines for determining whether and how its statutes apply, and whether the application requires any modification in existing rules. For example, does an investigation of human gene therapy that is supported by funds from the National Institutes of Health need to be reviewed by the RAC and also by the Food and Drug Administration under an investigational new drug application? The Food and Drug Administration must determine whether products containing genetically engineered microorganisms constitute food additives, drugs, or other products subject to their approval. The EPA must determine whether products are pesticides or industrial chemicals. The Department of Agriculture must determine whether products are plant pests, animal biologics, or agriculture products subject to its authority. It is expected that for some of these products agency statutes will provide overlapping authority. And here, the need for a well-defined mechanism for interagency coordination becomes evident.

A second common feature of the policy statements is that all

1. "Proposal for a Coordinated Framework for Regulation of Biotechnology," *Federal Register*, vol. 49 (December 31, 1984), pp. 50856–907.

three agencies will for now approach the review of biotechnology products and processes on a case-by-case basis, employing internal staff consultants and expert advisory committees. The safety of a product is of primary concern. The efficacy on a case-by-case basis may also be considered. Balancing the risks and the benefits is the ultimate job of the responsible agency.

It is also clear from the policy statements that with such an approach, agencies will develop expertise. A scientific data base that will facilitate subsequent review of other products of similar types and uses will be established. Communication and coordination between agencies concerning their historical experience, particularly for similar products under several agencies' jurisdiction, becomes an important element of a streamlined regulatory system. A vital part of each agency's policy statement is that each of the agencies (the Environmental Protection Agency, the Food and Drug Administration, and the Department of Agriculture) is committed to working together and with the other members of the cabinet council working group to coordinate both scientific evaluation and administrative procedures for biotechnology.

The obvious question is how does one institutionalize this commitment to coordinate decisionmaking of the agencies with their different missions, statutes, and agendas with regard to the scientific assessments of safety and benefits and with regard to the administrative procedures. The working group has proposed a two-component structure to accomplish this. One is a scientific advisory mechanism that is knit together by a strong interagency parent board and evaluates science and safety. The other is an interagency coordinating committee on risk management and regulation.

A new review mechanism

A strong scientific advisory mechanism is essential to the process of balancing risks and benefits. A sound scientifically based review of risks associated with a given process or product, which includes identification of areas of any scientific uncertainty, is needed. If there is any inadequacy in our federal structure for assessing safety of modern biotechnology, it is in the availability of a scientific review mechanism that can deal with a broad range of products now emerging and on the horizon. The RAC is neither equipped nor desirous of taking on that role on a governmentwide basis. Although much of the science that underlies review of commercial or agricultural products is the same, the RAC is oriented toward basic biomedical research and not commercial scale up and has limited environmental and ecological expertise. Nevertheless, a central core of scientific expertise for all the agencies would promote consistent assessments of risks key to any final risk-benefit analysis and key to a streamlined and consistent federal approach to biotechnology.

Accordingly, the working group proposes a two-tiered scientific review body composed of five agency-based scientific advisory committees (the Environmental Protection Agency, the Food and Drug Administration, the Department of Agriculture, the Recombinant DNA Advisory Committee, and the National Science Foundation) under a coordinating parent board composed primarily of members of the agency-based committees. The membership would include primarily nongovernment experts in scientific areas related to biotechnology. The agency-based committees will provide the detailed case-by-case scientific review of applications and will respond fully to the needs of the agencies regarding time constraints and proprietary and security procedures.

The parent board will be centrally located, will be informed of reviews being conducted by the agency committees, will review the final committee reports, and will, in time, be the group that develops generic scientific guidelines that can be applied to similar applications. The parent group will evaluate the review processes of the agency committees and conduct analyses of broad scientific concerns involving biotechnology. The central board will thus provide a framework for cooperation among the agencies on scientific issues and by it foster consistent decisionmaking. For example, broad issues related to research or commercial applications involving exchange of genetic material across species would be of common concern to the National Institutes of Health, the Food and Drug Administration, and the Department of Agriculture, at the least. A standing interagency scientific panel would be equipped to bring to bear the varied concerns and perspectives of the somewhat different scientific communities represented in the different agencies.

This scientific advisory mechanism is, however, advisory. It is geared to provide scientific assessment of risk and suggest guidelines for minimizing risk. It provides valuable information necessary to the regulatory process. It does not, however, make regulatory decisions, nor does it make the final assessments on balancing risks and benefits. The latter is the responsibility of the agencies. Their job is to carry out the law and take action under the authority granted to them by law.

Where then within this framework is the opportunity to coordinate and evaluate the existing and ongoing regulatory activities?

If one accepts that biotechnology is a new and emerging field that charts courses never dreamed by the legislators who wrote the authorizing agency legislation, one accepts that the statutes may not always be adequate or appropriate as times change. Accordingly, a means to evaluate the ongoing regulatory and decision-making framework; to suggest improvements in the current framework where necessary; and, to facilitate communication of decisions affecting biotechnology both within and outside government is needed.

Recognizing these needs, the cabinet council working group endorsed the establishment of an interagency coordinating committee on biotechnology. This committee would foster timely and coordinated decisionmaking by regular interagency communication on specific and general regulatory matters. This committee would also discuss issues of jurisdiction among agencies and serve as a forum by which agencies can raise public and industry concern. Further, it would consider general approaches for balancing risks and benefits and translating risk assessment information into policy decisions. The working group believes that existing authorities are adequate to deal with the products now emerging from modern biotechnology. However, the need for an ongoing mechanism to monitor the changing scene and to make appropriate recommendations for legislation or administrative action is also needed. At the present time the White House's cabinet council working group can serve these needs.

I have outlined a wide range of authorities and procedures that represent a coordinated federal framework for regulation of biotechnology. The effectiveness of the framework ultimately lies in those that give it life: the agencies that are committed to working with each other as they carry out their own responsibilities; the industries that are committed to good-faith dealings with the agencies and with the public; and the public itself, which comes to trust that the many benefits of biotechnology will be realized only in the context of safety for human health and the environment.

Comments by Donald S. Frederickson

IN LIGHT of current litigation concerning biotechnology before the courts, I have recently reread the National Institutes of Health guidelines on recombinant DNA research. In the revised guidelines that were first issued in 1977, I wrote a phrase that was forced upon me by Joe Califano (then secretary of Health, Education, and Welfare) and his many counsels, which said, "Under the revised guidelines, the NIH Director cannot approve proposed actions unless he determines that they present no risk to health or to the environment." After much struggle, I was allowed to add the word 'significant' before 'risk.' This anecdote indicates that there is a culture gap represented by the inability of legalisms to accommodate to stochastic processes.

Concerning the coordinated framework for regulation presented by Bernadine Bulkley, I have the following tentative reactions. First, the idea is based on a coordination of existing federal agencies. Those involved in biotechnology regulation need to be in agencies that are clearly answerable to the executive branch, are under congressional oversight, and within reach of the judicial process, if necessary. Only in this way will the balance of powers allow the fullest public access to the decisionmaking. Second, the decisions about laboratory research will continue to be made by research agencies, and regulation of products will fall to the regulatory agencies under their existing mandates. Third, coordination is to be provided by continuing cooperation among the federal science agencies and regulatory agencies.

There are going to have to be some practical requirements for all this to work. The coordination must be meaningful. There is a need for real leadership and for the development of ways to reach agreement upon jurisdiction. The regulatory process can be a source of a tremendous amount of inertia. Much of it is derived from the weight of ill-defined responsibility. A strong interest in the philosophical and the ethical aspects have to be maintained by all concerned, and this is just as important for the scientific elite as for those who make a profession of social concern. The care and responsibility for the preservation of the essential public interests have to be the first objective of all who participate in these new issues that are created by the new biology.

Comments by Douglas M. Costle

AT THE HEART of the problem of developing regulations for biotechnology that the public will accept is the scientists' ability to communicate to a broad lay audience in terms it can understand. It is impossible for an educated layperson not to get excited by the profound implications and potential benefits to society that can come from biotechnology. Also, for the average layperson, like many complicated scientific matters, biotechnology has a mystical aura about it. In today's society the transmission of knowledge and information has been greatly accelerated by technology. It is very hard for people to make sense of it all.

There are several things that will essentially frame the political discourse over the issue of biotechnology. Today, the priestly authority once given to experts has slowly eroded. Scientists do not come to the table value free; they bring their own values with them. It will not be sufficient for the scientific community to say, "Look folks, don't worry, we know what we are doing."

Second, it is clear that this technology will not enjoy a quiet incubation period that has often been given to other technologies in the past. It is going to be controversial from day one. The public will demand a seat at the table and will want to be part of the debate over the means and ends. They will not accept the simple assurance, "Don't worry, we know what we are doing."

The issue in the public's mind will be, "Do you know what you are doing, and have you taken the time and effort to persuade others of that?" There is a real opportunity right now to preempt friction and confrontation. Industry, scientists, and the university community must do their homework by laying an intellectual framework for decisionmaking that will persuade the public that its interest in health, safety, and the environment is being adequately protected.

Comments by Jonathan Lash

As THE DISCUSSION of potential biotechnology regulation opens, the unique aspects of the setting in which the discussion is taking place deserves comment. Potential regulation of an industry is being discussed without any evidence whatsoever that the industry has ever caused one shred of harm to human beings or to the environment. That is unique in our history. We are entering a discussion of potential regulation, partly at the suggestion of elements of the industry that is going to be regulated. That also must be unique.

We are entering a discussion of potential regulation without any clear idea of what the processes or products or risks are, because the field is moving so quickly and changing so fast. That necessarily leaves the discussion in a state of limbo. Another unique aspect of this debate is that a single public advocate, Jeremy Rifkin, has managed to unify the scientific, industrial, and regulatory communities in a combination of anger, resentment, and fear, while creating a public debate that mixes questions of ethics and questions of risks so inextricably that it is very difficult to separate them when one wants to approach a more limited discussion of regulation.

I want to discuss only one issue, the proposed approach to government regulation of this industry. How can possible risks be identified and controlled? Bernadine Bulkley said that the White House's Cabinet Council Working Group on Biotechnology operated under several premises. One premise is that biotechnology is good. I do not think it is government's role to say it is good or bad. In fact, that propels the debate into ethics and objectives that will obstruct a discussion of reduction of risk. The question is not whether the industry is good or bad; the industry exists and is proceeding. The question is, how can society ensure that the risks are minimized? This is a science that has enormous potential to benefit society, and some potential as yet unknown to do harm. It is appropriate for government to seek to learn about and to prevent that harm.

The administration has done something entirely reasonable, commendable, and really quite remarkable in making an effort to combine the agencies that could potentially deal with this issue, to get them to work together to assess the problem, to assess the existing legislation, and to determine what can be done, what has been done, and what should be done. I do not think that I have seen, in the years that I have been an environmental advocate, a similar cross-agency effort to assess the problem, and I think these agencies should be congratulated for trying.

Yet there are four criticisms of the proposed plan. First, there are marked differences in the agencies' approaches to biotechnology and its risks.[1] The Food and Drug Administration's statement says, "The Agency possesses extensive experience with the administrative and regulatory regimes described as applied products of biotechnology processes, new and old, and proposes no new procedures or requirements for the regulated industry or individuals."

The Environmental Protection Agency says, "A major common issue in this field is the need to determine what information is necessary for assessing the risks posed by non-indigenous and genetically engineered microorganisms. Although EPA has experience with regulating naturally occurring microbial pesticides, there is concern about potential human or environmental risks." The agency concludes that it knows much too little, does not

1. The agencies' statements are published in "Proposals for a Coordinated Framework for Regulation of Biotechnology," *Federal Register*, vol. 49 (December 31, 1984), pp. 5086–97.

know how to proceed, and will have to make some market changes in its approach in handling this new field.

Then there is the Department of Agriculture, which says that it anticipates that agriculture and forestry products developed by modern biotechnology will not differ fundamentally from conventional products. "We believe that the existing regulatory framework of USDA, combined with the NIH guidelines which are mandatory for all research grants, are adequate and appropriate for regulating research and development." The agencies have not decided on any common theme about whether there is any new and significant risks here or not. It will be difficult to develop any kind of a unified approach if there is a disagreement about whether there is really anything new, unique, or significant at issue.

My second criticism is that, because of the differing approaches of the three agencies, there is no consistent, defined approach to intentional releases. Will consistent data be collected before an experimental release; will consistent protocols be applied; will there be a consistent mode of assessment of any potential; and will there be consistent monitoring after release has taken place? This is not just a safety or risk issue. It is also a very important issue of economic fairness among different industries.

A third problem is the differing missions of the three agencies. The Environmental Protection Agency is a regulatory agency, and its mission under almost all of its statutes is to protect public health, safety, and the environment. The Department of Agriculture has a fundamental mission of enhancing and encouraging the agricultural industry. That is very different from the Environmental Protection Agency's mission and very different from the mission that it can be expected to undertake in regulating the process and products of biotechnology.

Finally, there is a product orientation in the notice in the *Federal Register*. The notice is about the regulation of products that will be made commercially available, and how to ensure their safety. It does not look at the manufacturing or research or experimentation process and make any determination of whether there are safety hazards there that should be regulated. I assume that the notion is that the National Institutes of Health Recombinant DNA Advisory Committee (RAC) guidelines, goodwill, and good sense will take care of that problem. I think that is a flawed notion.

Bernadine Bulkley said that there is rather ample federal authority to regulate biotechnology. Although the notice in the *Federal Register* describes many laws and regulations, nothing applies to the process between the RAC guidelines, application at the basic laboratory level, and the regulation of products. The Occupational Safety and Health Act is mentioned in the matrix of laws, but no action under the act is suggested; indeed, the Occupational Safety and Health Administration refused to participate in the *Federal Register* notice.

The Clean Air Act, the Clean Water Act, and the Safe Drinking Water Act are not even mentioned. The Resources Conservation and Recovery Act is mentioned, but no suggestion is made about how it might apply to the process.

Clearly, at this point there is no major problem with pollution from the biotechnology industry. The question is, will there ever be such a problem, and is there a potential for either intentional or accidental releases of products that could be dangerous to the environment? Are we creating a system in which the government will not have any data on that potential until it is too late?

Therefore, the *Federal Register* notice, in final form, must deal with the process of biotechnology, and must deal with how society can ensure that these will be zero discharge systems. There are two simple solutions—there can be no government regulation, or no industry. Everything else in between involves judgment and is going to be difficult.

Comments by Roger Salquist

I WOULD like to comment briefly from my perspective as the chief executive officer of a small, entrepreneurial company in this field about how I perceive the benefits, the risks, and then the proposed institutional framework for regulation. For the public debate to go forward, greater focus and clearer definition are needed. If the U.S. agricultural economy, which is still the largest part of the U.S. economy, is going to remain competitive, it must lower its costs and increase the value of its end products. Frankly, plant biotechnology is the only tool that is at hand for this and is a perceived benefit from this science, so there is a sense of urgency to apply this technology to agriculture.

The danger is, however, that the technology (if not the products) is going to leak overseas. The U.S. economy of the future is not based on smokestack industries; it is based on new technologies. If the United States lets technology go overseas, it is giving up major export markets of the future. One theme that has run consistently through the conversations that I have had in Europe during the past year has been the Europeans saying, "Look, we missed out on the electronic revolution. We weren't there in semi-conductors, and by God, we are not going to miss out on biotechnology." One can see initiatives all over the place right now over there to see that they do not miss out on biotechnology. One of the most innovative European nations is Holland, where a $280 million fund has been formed. The fund's objective is biotechnology. Overtures have been made to five of the leading U.S. companies in the various segments of biotechnology. The sole objective is to get that technical know-how into the laboratories and into commercial practice in Holland. One U.S. company, Centacor, has already made a commitment to go there.

The United Kingdom, on the other hand, has a rather different and unique approach. It has given the first right of refusal to all of the technology developed by its equivalent of the U.S. Agricultural Research Service, formed a company, and taken the company public on the basis of that leveraged technology. The money that the public invests is in turn used for research being done in the government labs. In an era of tight budgets, that is an innovative way to provide quick funding and to provide a commercial focus for that research.

To talk a minute about risks, I would submit that one must be specific and not talk so much about generalities. In the case of agriculture, I think the issue concerns whether there is a need to assess the impact on the life cycle of every species and organism in the state of California to determine the impact of putting some genetically engineered tomato or tobacco plants out in the field.

There are several fundamental questions to be asked, and I think the knowledge and the tools are already at hand to tell what the answers are. One, if a plant is put in the field with a new gene in it, what are the mechanisms and what is the likelihood that that gene can be transmitted nonsexually to other organisms? What are the vectors available for horizontal transfer? Frankly, my colleagues have done an exhaustive amount of work in this area and cannot find any. There are no proven cases where natural horizontal transfer in the case of plants has unequivocally been shown to occur.

The second issue is, what is the effect of that gene on the plant itself? What is the plant to which you have purposely introduced the gene going to do? In this case, science really does know more than many people are willing to admit.

For example, in the case of herbicide tolerance, a gene has been identified that confers resistance to one of the leading herbicides. That gene is well characterized, and it is known that there is one single nucleotide base pair change between that gene and the naturally occurring gene in the plant. Any single plant can be tested and in a matter of hours one knows exactly whether or not the gene is there, where that gene acts, and that it acts in a biochemical pathway that does not exist in humans. One can measure exactly how much of our recombinant enzyme and how much of the naturally occurring enzyme are functioning together in a plant at any time. There is, in fact, extremely detailed knowledge about the molecular level workings of the products that one is working with.

What about an institutional framework for regulation? As a small businessman in this field, I believe in pragmatic, timely, and flexible regulations. In my opinion, the regulations as published in the *Federal Register* are an excellent first step in that direction.

Comments by Jerry Caulder

THERE ARE two things that I would like to focus on that are important, and which on the surface appear to be mutually exclusive. These are intellectual property rights, and regulations. In the area of regulation two basic things must be done. One, make the regulations sufficiently broad. We do not know all the answers, we do not know what all the questions are going to be. And no one is going to be able to anticipate all the questions. So let us not get bogged down with details right now. Second, make the regulations flexible so that industry can develop those data needed to make commercial decisions. Those are not always the same as the data needed for registration of a product.

How do we accomplish the objectives of meeting the public's need to know what is going on with these new products and new technology while at the same time protecting industry's property rights? A small company really owns two things—intellectual assets, and the ability to create more intellectual assets. Those things need protection. But I also recognize the need for a small business to communicate to the public. Business must convince the public that it is doing useful, safe things, and that its products are properly regulated.

We now ask ourselves why we are not doing these things; they appear to be fairly simple objectives. Perhaps you remember when you were high school seniors and were not well prepared for a class. There was always one guy in the class that you could count on to start asking enough trivial questions that the class never got around to discussing what it needed to discuss. I think we have got a lot of high school seniors asking these questions now. And I can assure you that if those seniors ask these questions, there are going to be some problems.

So I would say if those questions continue, those rhetorical questions will bog us down on problems that are not real problems. The biotechnology industry will not get going where it needs to go in the time frame it has to get there.

Comments by Harvey S. Price

THREE highlights come out of this meeting. One concerns the tone of the debate. Another touches on whether the panelists have agreed on how to pursue the task of reducing unknowns. Finally, a slightly modified lesson can be drawn from the tradition of Asilomar and the National Institutes of Health, which has served the biotechnology community rather well in the last decade.

The question of tone can hardly be overrated. It is not only illogical but irresponsible to equate all unknowns with perils. This is a dialogue, not a debate. It is reasonable to eschew the traditional adversary mentality, in which one automatically puts industry in one corner, puts other forces in other corners, and assumes that by yelling and screaming reasonable results can be reached. This process was used in the 1970s, perhaps not without some benefit, but also with substantial detriment to the way society addresses important issues. Society can do better in the 1980s with biotechnology.

Second, while it is important to establish a predictive ecology, one must not be seduced into relying too heavily on a predictive model in an area in which there are tremendous uncertainties. A case-by-case analysis using human judgment is very important, and so is the experience to be gained from the initial experiments that are permitted to proceed.

Finally, the experience of Asilomar and the National Institutes of Health indicates that one should do the easy experiments first. That is, if you think of everything as one insolvable and indivisible problem, it is very difficult to get moving. But one can divide problems into different categories. One is more familiar with some things and less familiar with others, and some things seem inherently less dangerous than others.

Comments by Edwin H. Clark, II

IN SOME WAYS, biotechnology provides the twentieth century equivalent to the organic chemical revolution that started about one hundred years ago. That revolution brought immense benefits to society. But it also brought substantial risks and costs. I think no one would argue that society should not have benefited from those developments, but many wish that society had managed them better.

Yet biotechnology is really not the same as chemistry. Certainly the science is different; it is biology, not chemistry. More important, society is different. Society now takes a different view of the acceptability of risks, the omniscience of scientists, and the rights of innovators and producers. These changed perceptions have been incorporated in a series of laws, environmental requirements, and regulatory processes that define an entirely different social environment for such innovation. However, they do not guarantee an affirmative answer to the question: can society manage a technical revolution right this time? I hope so, for clearly there are substantial mistakes that can occur if not.

There are four basic types of mistakes. A type I mistake occurs when problems are identified that do not really exist. A type II mistake is failing to identify problems that do exist. A type III mistake is the unreasonable suppression of the benefits the innovations can provide because of too much concern about problems that may exist. Finally, the type IV mistake is failing to promote the benefits that the innovation could provide.

The challenge is to establish a social decisionmaking process that minimizes the cost associated with the four types of mistakes, and that remains robust in a scientific, social, legal, and political environment characterized by substantial uncertainty.

The 1975 Asilomar Conference and its aftermath made major contributions toward avoiding the type I mistake. However, this effort needs to continue, focusing now on the release of these organisms into the environment in addition to laboratory experiments. A critical first step in this process is the development of a topology of processes and organisms that will allow us to focus our attention on those that might truly offer problems and avoid raising impediments to the development of those that do not.

Avoiding the type II mistake requires the development of substantially improved assessment methodologies. These will have to cover indirect effects as well as direct effects, monitoring and containment as well as predictive capabilities, and testing as well as analytical protocols. The biological equivalent of the structural characteristics analysis being used by chemists to identify potentially toxic substances must also be developed. But other potential effects must be considered to ensure that seemingly beneficial innovations do not indirectly cause serious problems through ecological disruptions.

Avoiding the type I and type II mistakes will help substantially in avoiding type III. But something more will be required, and that is an honest and open public dialogue incorporating diverse professional perspectives, diverse social perspectives, and diverse concerns. The Asilomar approach—getting a group of very bright scientists together in a secluded spot to talk over the problems— is not sufficient to do the job. Government will be a major participant in these dialogues, but it will have to be a neutral government that invites wide public involvement in the process of identifying and resolving issues and making decisions; a government that can be trusted by all sides. If the U.S. government cannot play such a role, there will be a much greater risk of experiencing a type III mistake.

Avoiding the type III mistake will also be much easier if the type IV mistake is avoided, by setting up a process for identifying and promoting all the benefits that biotechnology can realistically bring. If the public perceives the innovations as providing something more than large corporate profits, it will be much more likely to accept the inevitable risks involved.

Avoiding all these mistakes is going to be a very frustrating process, one requiring patience, understanding, and goodwill on all sides. However, the alternative could be very expensive.

Agenda for the Future

SANDRA PANEM

THE CONFERENCE summarized in this volume has exposed the rich variety of questions pertinent to a formation of federal biotechnology policy. Chief among these are issues of public education and involvement, the extent and jurisdiction of regulation, the role and the state of the art of risk assessment, and the role of technical experts in establishing federal regulatory policy for biotechnology. While this list describes a full agenda, additional questions remain that also require attention. Together, those problems that have not yet been resolved and those not yet explored define the issues for future resolution.

The international aspects of biotechnology are among the issues not yet addressed. Biotechnology is fundamentally international in its scientific origins, the international way in which scientists are trained, and the multinational configuration of the corporations involved in the commercialization of biotechnology. The absence of significant representation of the international science and technology community at the January 1985 conference, and the questions that international realities present, are notable. The very same unique characteristics of biotechnology (viability of the products), which do not respect limitations of scale, do not respect geopolitical boundaries. The regulation of biotechnology provides a challenge and opportunity to establish an internationally consistent approach for an environmental regulatory program.

Several speakers noted some international concerns in passing as they relate to the world market for biotechnology products. Included were concerns about inconsistencies between U.S. laws and those of other nations that might force U.S. industry to invest in factories abroad. Harmonizing regulations and incentives among countries is clearly desirable for both economic and environmental reasons. International efforts to develop consistent international policy are now under way through the Organization for Economic Cooperation and Development, and the European Economic Community. Therefore, the issues surrounding international biotechnology—trade, cultural, legal, and scientific questions—define

90

a subset of public policy questions worthy of extensive and reasoned debate.

There are also a series of questions at the juncture of technology, law, and public policy that biotechnology epitomizes. As Judge David L. Bazelon has commented

> If agencies and legislatures fail to address the risks of biotechnology—either to deter them or compensate their victims—the courts will likely do so, perhaps even more vigorously, in deciding private lawsuits. . . .
>
> Regulation through the common law has many drawbacks. It has a substantial impact on science, technology, and the economy generally. It "regulates" and constrains just as surely as an agency does. It can cause researchers to follow a variety of unnecessary practices, simply to avoid lawsuits. It also imposes extremely high costs in damages, insurance, and attorneys' fees. Moreover, judicial regulation cannot provide the consistency, rationality, or political responsiveness offered by a consciously designed and clearly articulated legislative solution. A courtroom is not the place to decide such complex and controversial issues of fact and policy. And judges are not the appropriate persons to decide them.
>
> Although the appropriate role for the courts in the regulation of biotechnology is limited, it is nevertheless important. It consists principally of judicial oversight of actions by administrative agencies.[1]

Another area deserving attention is how the federal agenda for research in the basic biological sciences will be established. The biotechnology revolution of the 1970s has narrowed the distance between the endeavors of basic and applied research. Consequently, decisions about the training of life scientists and about what research will be done in university settings will have increasing importance for industry. Policies that shape the evolving relationships between academe, industry, and government must be continually monitored and questioned.

The addresses and comments that compose this volume have articulated the many questions now under discussion, as well as mentioning additional issues that should be explored. In the closing session, Robert Nicholas, a former congressional staff director, echoed a continuing theme, "We need to try to anticipate what the issues are and to develop the intellectual capital to respond to those issues, to formulate public policy before a crisis, before we are forced to do so. This conference has been one beginning."

1. David L. Bazelon, "Governing Technology: Values, Choices, and Scientific Progress," *Technology in Society,* vol. 5, no. 1 (1983), p. 19.

Glossary of Terms in Biotechnology

Antibody A protein (immunoglobin) produced by humans or higher animals in response to exposures to a specific antigen and characterized by specific reactivity with its complementary antigen. (*See also* monoclonal antibodies.)

Antigen A substance that, as a result of coming into contact with appropriate cells of the immune system, induces a state of sensitivity, often by the production of antibodies.

Artificial selection Techniques imposed on populations of organisms to favor the growth or multiplication of a particular organism.

Bacteria Any of a large group of microscopic or submicroscopic prokaryotic organisms having round, rodlike, spiral or filamentous, unicellular or noncellular bodies that are often aggregated into colonies; are enclosed by a cell wall or membrane; and lack fully differentiated nuclei. Bacteria may exist as free, living organisms in soil, water, and organic matter, or as parasites in the live bodies of plants, animals, and other microorganisms.

Biological product A virus, therapeutic serum, toxin, antitoxin, vaccine, blood, blood component or derivative, allergenic product, or analogous product used for the prevention, treatment, or cure of disease or injuries.

Biotechnology Biotechnology is the application of biological systems and organisms to technical and industrial processes.

Deliberate release The act of placing into the environment a microbe for a particular purpose (for example, pest control, depression of a plant's freezing point, or other reasons).

Gene The basic unit of heredity; an ordered sequence of nucleotide bases, comprising a segment of DNA.

Genome Genetic endowment of an organism or individual.

Gene pool Total genetic information possessed by a population whose members naturally exchange genetic information.

Gene therapy   The insertion of a gene into a patient so that it corrects a genetic defect.

Gene transfer   The use of genetic or physical manipulation to introduce foreign genes into host cells to achieve desired characteristics in progeny.

Genetic engineering   A technology used to alter the hereditary makeup of a living cell so that the cell can produce more or different chemicals or perform completely new functions.

Genetic material   DNA, genes, and chromosomes that constitute an organism's hereditary material; RNA in certain viruses.

Hybridoma   Product of fusion between a myeloma cell (which divides continuously in culture and is "immortal") and an antibody-producing cell. The resulting cell grows in culture and produces monoclonal antibodies.

Monoclonal antibodies (mabs);   Homogeneous antibodies derived from a single clone of cells; mabs recognize only one chemical structure. Mabs are useful in a variety of industrial and medical capabilities since they are easily produced in large quantities and have remarkable specificity.

Mutation   A permanent inheritable change in a DNA sequence or chromosome.

Nonindigenous organism   Organisms placed in environments where they are not native.

Nucleic acid   Linear polymer consisting of purines or pyrimidine bases bound to a ribose sugar (RNA) or a deoxyribose sugar (DNA), which is in turn bound to a phosphate group.

Pesticide   Any substance or mixture of substances intended for preventing, destroying, repelling, or mitigating any pest; and any substance or mixture of substances intended for use as a plant regulator, defoliant, or desiccant.

Pharmaceuticals   Products intended for use in humans, as well as in vitro applications to humans, including drugs, vaccines, diagnostics, and biological response modifiers.

Physical containment   Procedures or structures designed to restrict the release of viable organisms; degree of containment varies.

Plasmid   An extrachromosomal self-replicating circular piece of DNA.

Recombinant DNA   The hybrid DNA produced by joining pieces of DNA from different organisms or synthetic DNA together in vitro.

Conference Participants

with their affiliations at the time of the conference

Stanley H. Abramson
Environmental Protection Agency

A. Karim Ahmed
Natural Resources Defense Council

Nicholas Ashford
Massachusetts Institute of Technology

John K. Atwell
Department of Agriculture

Mary Anne Bach
House Subcommittee on Science, Research, and Technology

Robert Barnard, Esq.
Cleary, Gottlieb, Steen and Hamilton

Patricia Bauman
Conservation Foundation

Edwin L. Behrens
Procter and Gamble Co.

Orville G. Bentley
Department of Agriculture

Frederick S. Betz
Environmental Protection Agency

John E. Blodgett
Library of Congress

J. Grant Brewen
Allied Corporation

Bernadine Healy Bulkley
Office of Science and Technology Policy

Ronald E. Cape
Cetus Corporation

Will D. Carpenter
Monsanto Company

Jerry Caulder
Mycogen Corporation

Kim Christiansen
Office of Senator Lawton Chiles

Edwin H. Clark, II
Conservation Foundation

Mary E. Clutter
National Science Foundation

John Cohrssen
Council on Environmental Quality

Rita Colwell
American Society for Microbiology

Cheryl Coodley
Senate Subcommittee on Science, Technology, and Space

Douglas Costle
Wald, Harkrader, and Ross

Katherine Y. Cudlipp
Senate Committee on Environment and Public Works

Barbara J. Culliton
Science Magazine

Judy R. Curry
Department of Agriculture

Mary Ann Danello
Food and Drug Administration

Karen Darling
Department of Agriculture

J. Clarence Davies
Conservation Foundation

David K. Diebold
Department of Commerce

Allen J. Dines
Agracetus Corporation

John D. Dingell
Democrat of Michigan, Chairman, House Committee on Energy and Commerce

Jack Doyle
Environmental Policy Institute

Sidney Draggan
National Science Foundation

Christopher Duerksen
Conservation Foundation

Diane Dumanoski
Boston Globe

Dave Durenberger
Republican of Minnesota, Chairman, Senate Subcommittee on Toxic Substances and Environmental Oversight

Frederick A. Eustis, III
Biogen Inc.

James J. Florio
Democrat of New Jersey, Chairman, House Subcommittee on Commerce, Transportation, and Tourism

Donald S. Frederickson
Howard Hughes Medical Institute

Phyllis K. Freeman
House Subcommittee on Oversight and Investigation

Robert Friedman
Office of Technology Assessment

Robert A. Fuller
Johnson & Johnson

Val Giddings
Office of Technology Assessment

David Glass
BioTechnica International Inc.

J. Leslie Glick
Genex Corporation

Dan Glickman
Democrat of Kansas, Chairman, House Subcommittee on Transportation, Aviation, and Materials

Terri Goldberg
Committee for Responsible Genetics

Bernard D. Goldstein
Environmental Protection Agency

Albert Gore, Jr.
Democrat of Tennessee, Chairman, House Subcommittee on Oversight and Investigations

Carol Gronbeck
Genentech, Inc.

Michael Gross
Triton Biosciences Inc.

Bailey Guard
Senate Committee on Environment and Public Works

Leonard Guarraia
Monsanto Company

Anita Gunn
Mary Reynolds Babcock Foundation

Barbara B. Haas
National Wildlife Federation

Harold P. Hanson
House Committee on Science and Technology

Zsolt Harsanyi
Porton International

Daniel Hartl
School of Medicine, Washington University

Paul Hauge
Conservation Law Foundation

Mark A. Harwell
Cornell University

Henry C. Hayworth
Exxon Research & Engineering Co.

Steven Heinberg
Pierson, Ball, and Dowd

Ezra D. Heitowit
House Subcommittee on Science, Research, and Technology

Timothy J. Henry
Health Industry Manufacturers Association

Roger C. Herdman
Office of Technology Assessment

Fred Hoerger
Dow Chemical Company

Anne Hollander
Environmental Protection Agency

Gerald Hursh-Cesar
Intercultural Communications, Inc.

David A. Jackson
Genex Corporation

Fred Kagan
Upjohn Company

Edgar L. Kendrick
Department of Agriculture

David T. Kingsbury
National Science Foundation

Jane E. Kneedy
Monsanto Company

Jonathan Lash
Natural Resources Defense Council

Joshua Lederberg
Rockefeller University

Morris Levin
Environmental Protection Agency

Simon A. Levin
Cornell University

Pierre Longin
Monsanto Company

Bruce F. Mackler
Association of Biotechnology Companies

William Marshall
Pioneer Hi-Bred International Incorporated

Michael Mason
House Committee on Energy and Commerce

Jessica Mathews
World Resources Institute

Carl Mazza
Environmental Protection Agency

Douglas K. McCormick
Bio/Technology Magazine

David Mead
House Legislative Council

John W. Melone
Environmental Protection Agency

Henry I. Miller
Food and Drug Administration

Lee Miller
Monsanto Company

David T. Modi
DuPont Chemical Company

John A. Moore
Environmental Protection Agency

Robert B. Nicholas
House Subcommittee on Oversight and Investigations

John R. Norell
Phillips Petroleum Company

Michael S. Ostrach
Cetus Corporation

Ron Outen
Senate Environment and Public Works Committee

David Padwa
Agrigenetics Corp.

Sandra Panem
Environmental Protection Agency

Thomas L. Parker
Genetics Institute, Inc.

Seth Pauker
Biogen Research Corporation

David Pramer
Rutgers University

Harvey Price
Industrial Biotechnology Association

Frederick A. Provorny
Monsanto Company

Rana Quraishi
Office of Senator Gary Hart

Joseph W. Raksis
W.R. Grace and Co.

Edward W. Raleigh
DuPont Chemical Company

George B. Rathmann
Amgen

Ellen Riker
House Subcommittee on Health and Environment

Anthony Robbins
House Committee on Energy and Commerce

Michael Rodemeyer
House Committee on Science and Technology

Edward Lee Rogers
Rogers and Hamilton

James Rubin
Allied Corporation

Roger Salquist
Calgene Corporation

Frank E. Samuel, Jr.
Health Industry's Manufacturers Association

Harold M. Schmeck, Jr.
New York Times

Randal P. Schumacher
Chemical Manufacturers Association

Frances Sharples
Office of Senator Albert Gore, Jr.

George Shibley
Department of Agriculture

Hedy Sladovich
Meloy Laboratories, Inc.

Russell L. Smith
House Committee on Energy and Commerce

Martin Smith
White House Office of Policy and Development

Gerald G. Still
Department of Agriculture

Bernard Talbot
National Institutes of Health

Jim Tavares
National Academy of Sciences

Lewis Thomas
Memorial Sloan-Kettering Cancer Center

Ray Thornton
University of Arkansas

Sue A. Tolin
Virginia Polytechnic Institute and State University

Anne K. Vidaver
University of Nebraska

William T. Waugh
Environmental Protection Agency

Heather Wicke
Senate Committee on Environment and Public Works

Frank E. Young
Food and Drug Administration